F. SCOTT FITZGERALD

A LERNER BIOGRAPHY

F. SCOTT FITZGERALD

VOICE OF THE JAZZ AGE

CAROLINE EVENSEN LAZO

 Lerner Publications Company / Minneapolis

To the students of St. Paul Academy and Summit School

Acknowledgements: Special thanks to Paula Kringle for her kindness in assisting with this project, and to Leila Jackson Poullada for sharing her memories of her father, Norris D. Jackson, and his longtime friendship with F. Scott Fitzgerald.

Lerner Publications Company
A division of Lerner Publishing Group
241 First Avenue North
Minneapolis, MN 55401 U.S.A.

Website address: www.lernerbooks.com

Library of Congress Cataloging-in-Publication Data

Lazo, Caroline Evensen.
 F. Scott Fitzgerald : voice of the Jazz Age / by Caroline Evensen Lazo.
  p.   cm. — (Lerner biographies)
 Includes bibliographical references and index.
  Summary: Traces the troubled life of writer F. Scott Fitzgerald,
 from his spoiled, yet insecure childhood through his difficult
 marriage and writing career to his early death.
  ISBN: 0-8225-0074-4 (lib. bdg. : alk. paper)
  1. Fitzgerald, F. Scott (Francis Scott), 1896–1940—Juvenile
 Literature. 2. Authors, American—20th Century—Biography—
 Juvenile literature. [1. Fitzgerald, F. Scott (Francis Scott),
 1896–1940. 2. Authors, American.] I. Title. II. Series.
 PS3511.I9 Z676 2003
 813'.52—dc21   2001007210

Manufactured in the United States of America
1 2 3 4 5 6 – JR – 08 07 06 05 04 03

Contents

F. Scott Fitzgerald in 1919

Foreword

In letters he sent to young writers in the last years of his life, F. Scott Fitzgerald spelled out much that he had learned during his career.

To a teenager in Baltimore who had sent him a story of hers for his comments, he said, in effect, that she had to take the risk of putting her deepest and most personal feelings into her writing. "You've got to sell your heart, your strongest reactions, not the little minor things that only touch you lightly." That was the price of becoming a professional writer.

To a young student in Los Angeles who had composed a story that was "perfect technically and . . . absolutely sincere," Fitzgerald warned against the dangers of imitating great writers of the past. There was plenty to learn from Keats or Shakespeare or Dickens or Hemingway, but it was still more important to write in one's own voice.

To his daughter at Vassar, father Scott insisted on the virtues of discipline, hard work, and sticking to the task. "What little I've accomplished," he said, "has been by the most laborious and uphill work, and I wish now I'd never relaxed or looked back — but said at the end of *The Great Gatsby*: 'I've found my line — from now on this comes first.'"

It took Fitzgerald a long time to learn these lessons. Some of you who read his fascinating story may learn them more quickly.

Scott Donaldson,
Professor Emeritus
College of William and Mary

Introduction

No one would have guessed that a below-average, insecure student like F. Scott Fitzgerald would become one of America's greatest writers. And no one was more surprised by Scott's success than his former classmates at Saint Paul Academy in St. Paul, Minnesota, where his constant talking annoyed them. "If anybody can poison Scotty or stop his mouth in some way," a student wrote in the school paper, "the school at large and myself will be obliged."

Years later, Fitzgerald became famous for his wild lifestyle, which typified the upper echelons of American society in the 1920s. One of the amazing things about Fitzgerald, however, was his ability to withdraw from his wild life to write some of the most insightful and enduring fiction ever published in America.

The fact that Fitzgerald was a part of the lifestyle he wrote about gave his words the ring of truth and immediacy that endeared him to his readers. He showed little interest in the scientific or political achievements of the day. The new spirit of freedom after the end of World War I (1914 – 1918)— the freedom to improvise in life the way jazz artists did in music—drove his work.

Interest in Fitzgerald's life and work continues to brighten the literary world. New light focuses on his childhood—the strict teachings of the Catholic Church and how they later haunted his drive for material wealth. Fresh insights reveal the depth of his feeling of inferiority stemming from childhood classrooms and playgrounds. Critics continue to review his work—his masterpiece, *The Great Gatsby*, in particular. A leading critic concludes that it "may be the most widely read and admired American novel."

One-year-old F. Scott Fitzgerald stands in front of his childhood home in St. Paul, Minnesota.

ONE

The Dawn's Early Light

Ojibwa Indians were still camping on the banks of the Mississippi River when F. Scott Fitzgerald's maternal grandfather, Philip McQuillan, arrived in St. Paul, Minnesota. McQuillan, an Irish immigrant, opened a small grocery store and later made a fortune in the wholesale grocery business. He became known for both his wealth and his generosity—especially to the large Catholic community who attended St. Mary's Church and Visitation Convent School, both of which he cofounded.

McQuillan's wife, Louisa Allen, actively supported church and school projects and welcomed civic leaders, parishioners, and students to their home. By 1867 the McQuillan name was synonymous with hospitality, grace, and business leadership. The McQuillans were one of St. Paul's most admired families.

Scott's paternal grandfather, Captain Michael Fitzgerald, was an Irish Catholic, too, but he had settled in Maryland. His ancestors had first come to America in the 1600s, and he liked to boast that the Fitzgeralds were one of the oldest families in Maryland.

The home of Fitzgerald's maternal grandparents, Philip and Louisa McQuillan, in St. Paul's Lower Town

Like the McQuillans, the Fitzgeralds were devoted Catholics. In 1890, when their son, Edward Fitzgerald, married the McQuillan's daughter, Mollie, church activities and moral teachings played a prominent role in their lives as well.

Unlike his father-in-law, Edward Fitzgerald was not successful in the business world. Imbued with southern charm and a love of reading and drinking, he made friends easily. His dream of making a fortune in the furniture business, however, never materialized. Edward endured the embarrassment of depending on his wife's family to help support his own. Despite their financial woes, Edward and Mollie continued to live in the elegant Summit Avenue area of St. Paul, where the McQuillans were well established.

In this setting, their first and only son, Francis Scott Key Fitzgerald, was born on September 24, 1896. His two older sisters had died at the ages of one and three in an influenza epidemic during the summer of 1896. Overwhelmed with grief, both Mollie and Edward did their best to protect their son from the sadness they felt. Mollie could not help spoiling her only son, and she was determined to give him the best of everything—including a famous name. He was named after Francis Scott Key, a distant cousin who wrote the words to "The Star Spangled Banner." As he grew up, however, he preferred to be called Scott and to develop an identity all his own.

F. Scott Fitzgerald was named for Francis Scott Key, right, a distant cousin and composer of the lyrics to "The Star Spangled Banner."

*Fitzgerald as
an infant*

According to family records, Scott's first word was "up." While the word probably meant no more than a request to be lifted up by a parent, as toddlers typically use it, some believed he was already setting the direction of his life.

Mollie continued to dote on her son and, with the memories of her two daughters in mind, was especially concerned when fifteen-month-old Scott came down with a serious case of bronchitis. By the time he recovered, Edward's furniture store, American Rattan and Willow Works, closed for good, and he had to find a new job. Though the outlook seemed bleak, it brightened quickly when Edward received a job offer in the sales department of Procter & Gamble, a soap company in New York.

The Fitzgeralds lived in New York between 1898 and 1908. They moved to Buffalo with high hopes for Edward's success as a salesman. Yet soon after their arrival, tragedy struck the Fitzgeralds once again. Although Mollie's fourth pregnancy was full term, the baby died at birth. Finally in 1901, the family's wish came true when Annabel Fitzgerald was born, following their move to Syracuse, New York, where Edward continued as a salesman for Procter & Gamble.

Despite the family's recurrent financial troubles, Fitzgerald's parents gave their only son extravagant toys, such as this hobbyhorse.

*Fitzgerald's family had to move many times during his childhood.
Despite this hardship, he recalled his childhood fondly.*

Alhough Edward's job was adequate, he had a hard time maintaining the high standard of living the family had known in St. Paul and again needed financial support from the McQuillans. According to biographers David Page and John Koblas, Mollie wasted no time in using that support to pamper young Scott. "Mollie took advantage of the situation by spending winters with Scott in Washington, D.C.; sending him to Orchard Park, New York, where he caught a cold; packing him off for summer camp in Canada; and vacationing with him in the Catskill Mountains." She wanted him to have the best of everything.

Discipline was left to Scott's father, who sometimes beat his son if he didn't let his parents know his whereabouts or failed to come home at an appointed time. Nevertheless, Scott grew up with happy memories of listening to his father read to him and tell him Civil War stories. He admired his father's manners and the fine way he dressed. Scott did not feel the same way about his mother, whose appearance often embarrassed him.

Although Mollie was raised in the McQuillan style, her parents seemed to have neglected teaching her social skills and the flair for fashion that typified her mother and her friends. In fact, Mollie had often been treated as an outcast in the family's close-knit, elite St. Paul neighborhood, where one's looks and proper manners were important. As Scott grew older, such snobbery both fascinated and repelled him. He wanted desperately to be accepted by those who had "class" and material wealth, and at the same time he wanted to expose the emptiness of their lives.

Despite Scott's good looks and boundless energy, classmates quickly pegged him as the spoiled child that he was. He acted overconfident and conceited, yet his grades were low, and he made a poor showing in sports. He remained unpopular in school. Hoping to win friends, Scott made up stories to entertain the other children and even told lies to hold their attention.

Scott's early schooldays in upstate New York ended

This photo of ten-year-old Fitzgerald in his school uniform was taken while his family was living in Buffalo, New York.

abruptly in 1908 when his father lost his job. The blow devastated the family—especially Edward, whose only sure source of income was in St. Paul, where the McQuillans would pay for the children's education and allow the Fitzgeralds' high standard of living to continue. But after returning to Minnesota, a sense of insecurity hovered over the family and instilled in young Scott a lasting fear of poverty. He entered St. Paul Academy (SPA) with a "two-cylinder inferiority complex," as he called it. This stemmed in part from his father's image as a failure and his mother's reputation as an eccentric. Mollie was also the subject of local gossip that labeled her "frumpy."

But Scott did enter school with a certain confidence about his writing. Although he was unpopular because of his frequent talking and boasting, he finally received recognition for his talent. At the age of thirteen, Scott's first story, "The Mystery of the Raymond Mortgage," was published in *Now and Then*, a school publication that included interviews with nationally known figures. Scott seemed to have no doubt that he was on his way up since his work had been taken seriously, and his name was in print. His father's praise of the work encouraged him most of all.

Fitzgerald was already a published writer by the time he entered high school.

TWO

"That's Scott!"

While the mystery in "The Mystery of the Raymond Mortgage" was never completely solved, and any clues to great writing were barely visible, its publication meant a lot to Scott. He could hardly contain himself the day copies of the October 1909 issue came out. "I was so excited that I bounced in my seat and mumbled to myself, 'They're here! They're here!' until [others] looked at me in amazement." Seeing the story in print encouraged him to keep writing, and more stories, including "Read, Substitute Right Half," "The Room with the Green Blinds," and "A Debt of Honor" soon followed.

Scott's main goal at SPA, however, was to be a football star. Yet his height (five feet seven inches) and slight build, combined with his lack of athletic ability, hindered his chances of achieving greatness on the field. "In later gridiron contests he proved he had guts by expressing a desire to play despite a broken rib and other injuries," biographers have noted, "but determination alone was not enough for Fitzgerald to gain renown for handling the pigskin." Writing stories gave him a taste of the success that eluded him on the football field.

Fitzgerald and his family lived in the Summit Avenue neighborhood of St. Paul, pictured here in 1916.

Not everything printed in school publications pleased Scott. When a student's plea for "someone to poison Scotty or stop his mouth in some way" was published, his unpopularity at school seemed to be confirmed. But he had many friends in the Summit Avenue neighborhood—boys and girls alike. Janey Ingersoll called him "very attractive, bright, likable," and "good company." She had met Scott in a dancing class she organized with other neighborhood parents. Though the boys usually dreaded the classes, the girls enjoyed them, and the girls looked forward to dancing with Scott. He easily charmed them with his fine manners, fun-loving spirit, and good looks. His dancing partners included Alida Bigelow, Marie Hersey, Jean Ingersoll (Janey's daughter), and Kitty Ordway—all of whom were offspring of St. Paul's founding families.

On weekends in St. Paul, Scott and his friends went to movies and later played games in their backyards. The Charles Ames's house was a favorite, because it boasted a magnificent tree house behind the twenty-one-room mansion. Scott and Norris "Nonnie" Jackson often played there. Sometimes Scott liked to forget his fine manners and taunt the girls in his neighborhood. "During those SPA years, his sister Annabel was playing with a neighborhood girl on her back steps. . . . Without warning, a lean, long-legged boy jumped from the porch, directly over their heads and rushed on his way.

This portrait was taken during Fitzgerald's high school years. His attendance at exclusive schools such as St. Paul Academy and the Newman School fueled his fascination with the trappings of wealth.

He was out of sight before they could catch their breath. The astonished neighbor looked at Annabel, waiting for an explanation. Annabel met her gaze and answered, 'That's Scott!' "

Looking back on his teens, Fitzgerald revealed a quieter, more thoughtful attitude regarding girls: "I always had a secret yen for the lovely Scandinavian blondes who sat on porches in St. Paul but hadn't emerged economically to be part of what was then Society. They were too nice to be "chickens" [girls that kissed] and too quickly off the farmlands to seize a place in the sun, but I remember going round blocks to catch a single glimpse of shining hair—the bright shock of a girl I'd never know."

In 1911 Scott left SPA in a flurry of fun, writing and acting in plays that brought him the attention he craved. One of his biggest fans was Marie Hersey from his dance class. She was his first serious girlfriend.

Some descendants of old St. Paul families heard rumors that Scott had been a troublemaker in school, critical of others, boastful, generally unpopular, and that he was finally expelled from SPA. Although his grades were low, there is no proof that he was expelled from the school. His parents had enrolled him at the Newman School, a Catholic prep school in New Jersey, where he prepared to enter Princeton University, the prestigious Ivy League college in that state.

At the Newman School, Scott met the same criticisms that had plagued him at SPA—that he was conceited, boastful, and a lazy student. Scott did manage to play intramural football at Newman, and he attended some Broadway plays and musicals in nearby New York on weekends. The more knowledge about theater the better, he thought, because he had hopes of becoming a member of Princeton's Triangle Club, well known for its musical comedies. Scott even wrote

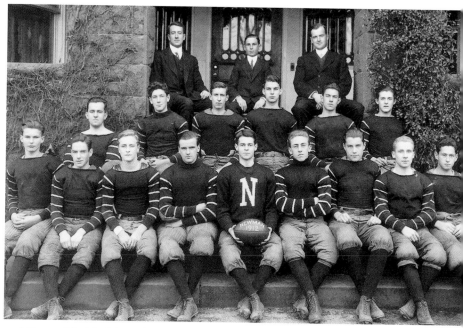

Fitzgerald, third from left in the bottom row, *realized his dream of playing football while at the Newman School in New Jersey.*

a play called *The Captured Shadow,* which was a mystery performed by the Elizabethan Dramatic Club, a local theatrical club in St. Paul, during his summer vacation in 1912.

The play was a success, and the cast, including Scott, who played the lead role of the crook, received rave reviews. He spent the rest of that summer with friends at their summer cabins on White Bear Lake, about twelve miles outside St. Paul, and with his aunt and uncle, Lorena and Philip McQuillan, at nearby Bald Eagle Lake. The lake area provided an idyllic summer scene with large cabins and sprawling green lawns that stretched down to the shore, and sailboats usually bobbing in the distance. Scott spent many hours there, daydreaming and basking in the sun.

Fitzgerald, age sixteen

Returning to Newman the following fall, Scott tried to raise his grades to assure his admission to Princeton but failed to do so. While at Newman, however, he did succeed in meeting two special people—Father Cyril Sigourney Fay and writer Sir Shane Leslie. Both became mentors and close friends. Fay was like a second father to Scott, and according to biographer Matthew Bruccoli, "encouraged his ambitions for personal distinction and achievement." Leslie also encouraged Scott's writing goals and, like Fay, reawakened his early connection to the Catholic Church. "He was a convert to the church of my youth," Scott wrote about Leslie, "and he and another [Fay] . . . made the church a dazzling, golden thing, dispelling its oppressive mugginess."

But Fitzgerald soon learned that it would take more than his writing skills and the influence of others to be admitted to Princeton. Only one person could accomplish that goal, and that was Scott himself. Classmates were quick to remind him that college was one place he could not talk his way into. Or could he?

At twenty-five cents per ticket, Fitzgerald's play The Coward *was a sell-out and raised $150 for the Baby Welfare Association.*

THREE

A Time to Fail...
A Time to Succeed

During the following summer, Scott's play *The Coward* was performed by the Elizabethan Dramatic Club. The production delighted audiences in both St. Paul and White Bear Lake and even earned front-page coverage in local newspapers. But the summer also marked the death of Louisa McQuillan, Scott's grandmother, who had given so much of her life to the community. Her estate, divided among the family, included funding for Scott's college education, which would begin on completion of his senior year at Newman.

In his last year at Newman, Scott took his first alcoholic drink, and later recorded in his *Ledger* (his diary) that he got "tight" from "four defiant Canadian Club whiskeys." But he often exaggerated such escapades—especially while home on school vacations. Scott celebrated his last Christmas vacation from Newman by going to parties and dances, but he knew the fun would soon end and he would face more testing on his return to school.

Having failed the first college entrance tests, Scott hoped to pass the makeup exam and be admitted to Princeton. (His friend Nonnie Jackson had been accepted at Princeton, and Scott was determined to join him there.) But once again, he failed. Finally, he decided to confront the admission officers and plead his case, which was based on his longtime dream of attending the prestigious school and on his confidence that he could do well there. Besides, he told them, it was his seventeenth birthday that day! His application was reviewed again, and Scott finally won admission to Princeton. Scott Fitzgerald, always berated by his classmates for talking too much, had talked his way into college. He telegraphed his parents to "send football pads and shoes immediately."

Fitzgerald set his sights on prestigious Princeton University, shown here in 1909, and would not give up until he had gained admission.

Fitzgerald, back row center, *was a member of the board for Princeton's literary magazine, the* Tiger.

Although Scott's good looks were striking and his verbal skills were superb, his ability to play football was neither. As in prep school, his weight (138 pounds) and small build still worked against him. So, as he had done in the past, he focused on his writing—this time for the Triangle Club and the *Tiger,* a Princeton literary magazine with a humorous slant. His academic record worsened because he devoted most of his time to writing and socializing. When he was invited to join the Cottage Club, an exclusive eating club, his extracurricular life became even more active. The eating clubs "marked the pinnacle of social success at Princeton," according to Professor Scott Donaldson. "Few underclassmen understood as thoroughly as Fitzgerald the character of the various clubs and their relative rank on campus."

Despite his love of talking about himself and his dreams of success, Fitzgerald made some good friends at Princeton, including Edmund Wilson, then literary editor of the *Tiger,* and John Peale Bishop, a poet. Bishop shared with Scott his love of Shakespeare, Keats, and other literary giants. Soon, Scott was writing a variety of pieces for the Triangle Club and was given full membership in the club. Scott once confided to Wilson, "I want to be one of the greatest writers that ever lived, don't you?"

Scott's preoccupation with writing and related activities took its toll when it came time for exams. His grades dropped so dramatically that he became ineligible for the presidency of the Triangle Club—a position he dearly wanted. "What an idiot I was to be disqualified . . . by poor work when men of infinitely inferior capacity got high marks without any great effort!" he later wrote.

During the summer of 1914, Scott returned to St. Paul to act in his play *Assorted Spirits.* The play is about a man who tries to convince a homeowner that his house is haunted so that he can buy it at a lower price. The play, Scott's last for the Elizabethan Dramatic Club, attracted attention from the press for more than the usual reasons. In an encore production at the White Bear Yacht Club, all the lights went out due to a blown fuse. To prevent panic, Scott "leaped to the edge of the stage" and calmed the audience with an ad-lib monologue. At the age of seventeen, Scott demonstrated the aplomb of a skilled professional.

Because of low grades, Scott's extracurricular activities were again curbed, and he was not allowed to act in the Triangle Club play *Fie! Fie! Fi-Fi,* which was a great success.

The play was memorable because it introduced the term *flapper* to describe a young girl who flaunted conventional behavior. The word became a permanent part of the English language.

In early January 1915, at the end of Christmas vacation, Scott met Ginevra King, Marie Hersey's roommate at Westover School in Middlebury, Connecticut. Scott and Ginevra were attracted to each other immediately, but she was also attracted to other young men. Scott was captivated by her charm, and he continued to write to her for months after returning to Princeton.

Due to his low grades at Princeton, Fitzgerald was unable to perform in Fie! Fie! Fi-Fi! *or in any of his other plays written for the Triangle Club.*

Fie! Fie! Fi-Fi!

A·MUSICAL·COMEDY·IN·
△ TWO·ACTS △
Presented by the
PRINCETON UNIVERSITY
TRIANGLE CLUB

Music by
D·D·Griffin'15 A·L·Booth'15 P·B·Dickey'17
Lyrics by
F·Scott·Fitzgerald'17

The John Church Co.
CINCINNATI
NEW YORK   LONDON

Fitzgerald's first love, Ginevra King, was the inspiration for many of his female characters.

On his return to college, Scott wrote the lyrics for *The Evil Eye*, a musical written by his friend Edmund Wilson for the Triangle Club. His academic record continued to prevent his full participation in such events (he had been cast as the female lead), but the Triangle Club's tour with *The Evil Eye* was a success in Chicago, St. Paul, and Minneapolis during the Christmas holiday season.

Scott had become ill over Christmas and stayed in St. Paul to recuperate. Bad news from Princeton—that he would have to repeat his junior year because of his poor academic record—lengthened his stay through the winter and spring of 1916. To lift his spirits, Scott attended a fraternity dance at the University of Minnesota in February disguised as a woman. When men started to flirt with him, he flipped off his wig and the men quickly vanished. The escapade was leaked to the *St. Paul Daily News*. Scott and his friends loved the attention, but he knew that his talent could be put to better use at Princeton for the Triangle Club, and he was anxious to return.

When Scott returned to Princeton in September 1916, he wrote the lyrics for *Safety First*, which was produced by the Triangle Club in December. He also worked on several stories, including "The Spire and the Gargoyle" and "Babes in the Woods" (based on his meeting Ginevra King), published in the *Nassau Literary Magazine (Nassau Lit)*. By then, he had recovered from his illness, an inactive case of tuberculosis, and felt much better. But his relationship with Ginevra was ending, and the rejection hit him hard, as Scott Donaldson noted in *Fool For Love*: "The hurt of losing her never left him, and thinking about it brought tears to his eyes . . . . Ginevra King, in short, was the golden girl that Fitzgerald . . . could not have." In January 1917, he noted in his *Ledger*, "Final break with Ginevra."

This portrait of Fitzgerald was taken while he was stationed at Camp Sheridan near Montgomery, Alabama.

FOUR

Lost and Found

Was it a vision, or a waking dream?
Fled is that music:——do I wake or sleep?
　　　　　　　　　　　　　—John Keats

F. Scott Fitzgerald was attracted to many young women in his youth, but failing to win Ginevra King meant waking from a dream he had had since his dancing-school days in St. Paul. She represented the spoiled rich girls that were an integral part of the upper-class environment he both craved and scorned. She was from a prominent family in Lake Forest, Illinois ("The most glamorous place in the world," he called it then), and she had the social status Scott had always wanted. Scott continued to think about Ginevra over the years and always perked up when he heard news of her. "Ginevra engaged?" he noted in his *Ledger* (June 1917), and, finally, "Ginevra married."

The United States entered World War I on April 6, 1917. Scott danced, partied, played golf, and learned to drive his father's car during the summer of 1917, but his frivolous spirit was soon dampened by the war effort. Scott decided to join the army rather than continue at Princeton after his junior year. In July 1917, he applied for an infantry commission at Fort Snelling, Minnesota. In the meantime, he worked on more stories for the *Nassau Lit.* and on a novel titled *The Romantic Egotist*, a story about a boy "growing up" at Princeton.

His commission came through on October 26, and he started training at Fort Leavenworth, Kansas, in November. Scott hoped to go overseas and win glory on the battlefield—the kind of glory he had dreamed about on the football field. While waiting for his overseas assignment, he spent his spare time at the Officers Club—alone at a table, writing his novel. He worked frantically to finish it. He was sure he would be killed in the war, and he wanted to leave something of value to mark his life. When he finally completed the manuscript, he gave it to his friend Shane Leslie for editing before sending it to Charles Scribner's Sons, a publishing house. Then Scott and his unit went to Louisville, Kentucky, and Camp Gordon in Georgia before moving on to Camp Sheridan, near Montgomery, Alabama—his last U.S. assignment.

Through friends at Princeton, Scott met and dated many young women while in the army. On one hot summer night in July 1918, he met a stunning southern belle named Zelda Sayre during a dance at the Montgomery Country Club. The petite seventeen-year-old with the rose pink coloring and red gold hair immediately caught Scott's eye. A few months later, he noted in his *Ledger*, "Fell in love [with Zelda] on the 7th."

Scott seemed to have found a new golden girl. In some ways Zelda was like Ginevra, but there was one big difference.

At the dance where Fitzgerald first met Zelda Sayre, above, other officers vied for her attention. Some pilots even flew stunts over her house until stopped by their commander.

Zelda, though self-centered and demanding, had not been raised with the trappings of great wealth. She was the daughter of Alabama Supreme Court judge Anthony D. Sayre and Minnie Sayre. Scott and Zelda were very much alike. In Zelda, Scott could see his own reflection.

Minnie Sayre doted on Zelda as a child just as Mollie Fitzgerald had doted on Scott. Minnie nurtured Zelda's free-spirited personality and even named her after a gypsy in *Zelda's Fortune*, one of Minnie's favorite books. But Scott also saw Zelda's tough drive for success and her fear of poverty.

Just as Scott was preparing to go overseas, World War I ended—on November 11, 1918—and he was discharged from the army. At the same time, he received news of Father Fay's death. "He was the best friend I had in the world," Scott wrote in a letter to Shane Leslie. His thoughts then turned to Zelda in whom he placed his faith and hope. He left Camp Sheridan, moved to New York City, and sent Zelda a telegram: DARLING HEART...I AM IN THE LAND OF AMBITION AND SUCCESS AND MY ONLY HOPE AND FAITH IS THAT YOU MY DARLING HEART WILL BE WITH ME SOON.

Scott and Zelda became engaged, and Scott took a job with an advertising firm in New York in hopes of earning enough money to support them when they married. They loved the excitement of New York's night life—the freedom and joy that permeated the postwar era and the jazz bands that kept people dancing until dawn. But Scott's income from advertising could not sustain the lifestyle he and Zelda craved, and Scribner's had rejected his novel. He would revise it, of course, but Zelda broke off their engagement. She did not want to risk poverty and failure. Scott returned to St. Paul to work on the book, determined to see it published and to marry Zelda.

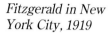

Fitzgerald in New York City, 1919

Mollie and Edward Fitzgerald had moved to a large house on Summit Avenue, and they reserved the third floor for Scott. It was a perfect place to work. His parents gave him complete privacy, tried to keep his friends away from the house, and to keep their own curiosities from interfering in Scott's business. While writing, Scott stayed away from alcohol. He wanted nothing to muddle his thinking or to shift his focus from his writing.

Maxwell E. Perkins, perhaps the most revered trade publishing editor of the first half of the twentieth century, adhered to standards of integrity, craftsmanship, and artistry.

While staying at his parents' house, Scott received no money from them, so he borrowed from his childhood friend Richard "Tubby" Washington. For literary advice, he went to Father Joe Barron, dean of students at St. Paul Seminary—a longtime recipient of donations from Annabel McQuillan, Scott's aunt. Barron was an author, and he and Scott became good friends.

In September 1919, Scott finished revising his novel and again sent it to Scribner's, where it was accepted by editor Maxwell Perkins. It was retitled *This Side of Paradise* and, to Scott's great relief, was to be published on March 26, 1920. Because he received no advance payment for his manuscript, Scott went to work immediately on some of his previously rejected stories and sold them to the *Smart Set*, a magazine that influenced literary taste in America at that time. It was edited by George Nathan and well-known critic H. L. Mencken. Scott also sent a few stories to *Scribner's Magazine*. *Scribner's* featured both well-known and unknown writers of fiction, nonfiction, poetry, theater reviews, photographic essays, and current events. Prices paid for stories in those days ranged from $35 to $150. Could income from sales of his stories support Scott and Zelda's lifestyle? Could he count on the success of his first novel? Money questions continued to mount.

Scott's financial worries quickly eased when a St. Paul friend recommended him to the Paul Revere Reynolds Literary Agency in New York. Harold Ober, a partner in the firm, agreed to represent Fitzgerald. Wasting no time, Ober sold Scott's story "Heads and Shoulders" to *The Saturday Evening Post*. The magazine, the most popular of its kind at the time, offered two hundred pages of fiction and articles of general information. At last Scott thought he could offer Zelda a bright future.

Fitzgerald courted Zelda actively, but she did not accept his offer of marriage until This Side of Paradise *was published.*

FIVE

Words of Wisdom

The wise writer, I think, writes for the youth of his own generation, critics of the next, and the schoolmasters of ever afterward.
—F. Scott Fitzgerald

In the third-floor sanctuary of his parents' house, Scott completed more stories, including "The Ice Palace," a story about a southern belle who visits her fiancé in Minnesota and nearly dies when she gets lost in a palace made of ice. He also wrote "The Camel's Back," his first story to be included in the O. Henry Prize Stories series, named after the esteemed American writer (1862–1910) whose short stories were known for their unexpected endings and use of coincidence. With his continued success, Scott made plans to win back Zelda.

In January 1920, Scott moved to New Orleans, Louisiana, to avoid the extreme cold in Minnesota and the risk of another round of tuberculosis. He found a quiet rooming house where he could write—not only stories but letters to Zelda. With the $600 he received from the O. Henry Prize, he bought her a platinum-and-diamond watch. With the gift in hand, Scott went to Montgomery and asked Zelda to marry him. She promised to do so as soon as *This Side of Paradise* was actually published that spring.

Fitzgerald lived briefly in a cheap boardinghouse in New Orleans' Garden District, pictured here about 1915.

Scott and Zelda in Montgomery, Alabama, 1921

"Her reconsideration was not entirely a mercenary matter," Matthew Bruccoli explains. "She was not committing herself to a famous and wealthy author. The reception of his novel was uncertain and neither of them had any idea what Fitzgerald's income would be. Zelda responded to his regained confidence, to his ability to fulfill his ambitions."

Meanwhile, Scott and Zelda continued to exchange love letters. In February, after Scott's visit, Zelda wrote: "Our fairy tale is almost ended, and we're going to marry and live happily ever afterward . . . . I do want to marry you even if you think I 'dread' it . . . I'll always be very, very happy with you— except sometimes when we engage in our weekly debates— and even then I rather enjoy myself. I like being very calm and masterful, while you become emotional and sulky. . . . I miss you so . . . I love you so. . . . "

That same month, Scott wrote to Isabelle Amorous, the sister of a Newman classmate. She had praised him when his engagement to Zelda was called off:

> No personality as strong as Zelda's could go without getting criticisms and as you say she is not above reproach. I've always known that. Any girl who gets stewed in public, who frankly enjoys and tells shocking stories, who smokes constantly and makes the remark that she has "kissed thousands of men and intends to kiss thousands more," cannot be considered beyond reproach even if above it. But Isabelle I fell in love with her courage, her sincerity and her flaming self respect and it's these things I'd believe in even if the whole world indulged in wild auspicions [sic] that she wasn't all that she should be. But of course the real reason, Isabelle, is that I love her and that's the beginning and end of everything.

Scribner's published *This Side of Paradise* in March 1920, and it brought instant fame to Fitzgerald. The first printing of three thousand copies sold out in three days. On April 3, Scott and Zelda were married in the vestry of New York's St. Patrick's Cathedral. It was a small ceremony, and neither Scott's nor Zelda's parents attended the wedding. Zelda's sister Rosalind Smith and Scott's Princeton friend Ludlow Fowler formed the wedding party. In typical unconventional form, Scott and Zelda planned no reception and took off for the Biltmore Hotel immediately after the ceremony.

This Side of Paradise *went through four printings in 1920, totalling forty-five thousand copies.*

While in New York, Scott and Zelda celebrated with Princeton friends, partied until dawn, and were even asked to leave hotels because of the disturbances they caused. Tales of Zelda dancing on tabletops and Scott riding on the hood of a taxi filled New York's gossip columns. At twenty-four, Scott was a famous author married to a beautiful and vibrant woman. Together they were the toast of the town. On the way to one party, it was reported, Scott "burst into tears, because he knew he would never again be so happy."

Scott and Zelda shortly after they were married

*John G. Hibben,
president of Princeton
University in 1920*

But back at Princeton, President John G. Hibben was in no mood to celebrate the publication of Scott's book. He objected to Fitzgerald's portrayal of Princeton as a "country club" where "young men are merely . . . spending their lives wholly in a spirit of calculation and snobbery." (In the novel, Amory's friend Tom sums up his years at Princeton: "I'm sick of adapting myself to the local snobbishness of this corner of the world. I want to go where people aren't barred because of the color of their neckties and the roll of their coats.")

In his reply to the president's criticisms, Scott explained: "I don't mean at all that Princeton is not the happiest time in

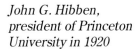

most boys' lives. It is of course—I simply say it wasn't in mine
.... I simply wrote out of my own impressions ... as honestly
as I could."

This Side of Paradise continued to resonate with readers
throughout the country. They saw in the writing the honesty
and beauty that made Fitzgerald unique:

> Long after midnight the towers and spires of
> Princeton were visible, with here and there a late-
> burning light—and suddenly out of the clear darkness
> the sound of bells. As an endless dream it went on; the
> spirit of the past brooding over a new generation, the
> chosen youth from the muddled, unchastened world,
> still fed romantically on the mistakes and half-
> forgotten dreams of dead statesmen and poets. Here
> was a new generation, shouting the old cries, learning
> the old creeds, through a revery of long days and
> nights. ... a new generation dedicated more than the
> last to the fear of poverty and the worship of success.

Fitzgerald's book became so popular that an abridged
edition was serialized in the *Chicago Herald and Examiner*,
the *Atlanta Georgian*, and the *New York Daily News*. In an
interview for *Scribner's*, Scott said: "I want to be able to do
anything with words. ... As a matter of fact, I am a professed
literary thief, hot after the best methods of every writer in my
generation."

Fitzgerald followed his first novel with a book of short
stories titled *Flappers and Philosophers*, published in
September 1920. But Scott needed a quiet place to continue
writing—away from New York's social whirlwind. Living in
costly hotels, buying expensive clothes, and paying for all-
night parties quickly depleted his income. Scott and Zelda
rented a cottage in Westport, Connecticut, where life, they
thought, would be calmer. It wasn't. Friends followed the

magnetic couple to their hideaway, and the partying continued.

Early that spring, Zelda discovered she was pregnant. The time was right, she thought, for a trip to Europe before motherhood began. Scott worked hard and fast to finish his second novel, *The Beautiful and Damned.* He needed money in the bank to pay for the trip. There seemed to be no desire to change their way of living, especially with so much to look forward to and so much to celebrate—their first trip abroad, a second novel in the works, and a baby on the way!

Fitzgerald and his new bride became the center of attention at social gatherings in both the United States and Europe.

SIX

What So Proudly We Hail

Scott and Zelda sailed to Europe on the ocean liner *Aquitania* and arrived in England in May 1921. While in London, they met Winston Churchill, future prime minister of England, and his wife, Lady Randolph Churchill. Zelda charmed Winston Churchill, and the two talked at length. Max Perkins had arranged for the Fitzgeralds to meet some of Great Britain's literary giants, including John Galsworthy, whose best-known work is *The Forsyte Saga*.

Similarities between Galsworthy and Fitzgerald abound in their writing. Both authors wrote about the "comfortable, secure, smug" eras in their respective countries. Both dealt with the consequences of impulsive behavior, and both lamented the dreams that did not last. Fitzgerald was so moved by Galsworthy's stories that he urged Scribner's to include some of them in a volume of short stories. Fitzgerald did not fear competition, he welcomed and promoted it.

The USS Aquitania *sailed to Cherbourg, France, before continuing on to Southampton, England.*

In Italy, Scott and Zelda made a pilgrimage to Rome, where John Keats is buried. Keats had been one of Scott's idols ever since his days at the Newman School. Two of Scott's favorite poems by Keats were "Ode to a Nightingale" ("which I can never read through without tears in my eyes") and "Ode on a Grecian Urn" ("unbearably beautiful, with every syllable as inevitable as the notes in Beethoven's Ninth Symphony").

After a month in Italy, Scott and Zelda returned to London for the British publication of *This Side of Paradise*, but the reviews were far less favorable than those in America. In fact, some reviewers called it "trivial and unconvincing," although the book was still popular in the United States. Once again, the Fitzgeralds thought it was time to move on.

Scott and Zelda decided to return home to await the birth of their baby. After a brief visit to Montgomery, Alabama, during the heat of the summer, Zelda and Scott moved back to Minnesota. "St. Paul," he told the *Daily News*, "is a nice quiet town to write [in]." White Bear Lake seemed especially inviting to the couple as the hot summer wore on. They moved into a summer cottage there in August, but again peace and quiet eluded them.

Scott's arrival was hailed like a hero's return home. Newspapers echoed what all his old friends were saying: "Fitzgerald's back in town!" As word spread, visitors wasted no time in greeting the illustrious couple. Nonnie Jackson, who was staying at the White Bear Yacht Club for a few weeks, joined friends from the old neighborhood—Marie Hersey, Alida Bigelow, and others—for rounds of theater openings and dinner parties in St. Paul.

Local media covered the famous author's literary accomplishments with great pride. The *St. Paul Daily News* announced that Scott had had a major novel and book of short stories published and a new book on the way "all in less than three years." Zelda, however, did not receive the warm welcome she may have expected. She had been the belle of the ball in Montgomery, but she was viewed as an outsider in the close-knit society of St. Paul. Scott's sister Annabel, however, thought Zelda was "the most beautiful woman in the world," and his mother agreed.

Both Scott and Zelda enjoyed cracking the facade of the buttoned-down community of the "proper" Midwest, but Scott

Fitzgerald did some important writing while in St. Paul, including many short stories. Throughout his career, he would publish more than 160 short stories.

worked hard writing, too. In addition to his revisions on *The Beautiful and Damned*, he wrote "Two for a Cent" and "The Diamond as Big as the Ritz," one of his most famous stories. In his foreword to *The Short Stories of F. Scott Fitzgerald*, Charles Scribner III summed up the author's special "enchantment" exemplified by "The Diamond":

> The key to Fitzgerald's enduring and elusive enchant-
> ment lies, I believe, in the power of his romantic
> imagination to transfigure his characters and set-
> tings—and indeed the very shape and sound of his

prose. I shall never forget that evening train ride…on which I first read "The Diamond as Big as the Ritz": a commute was converted into a fantastic voyage….The ultimate effect, once the initial reverberations of imagery and language have subsided, transcends the bounds of fiction.

But Scott spent most of the summer and fall enjoying social events and drinking too much at some of them. On August 25, 1921, Scott wrote to Max Perkins: "I'm having a hell of a time because I've loafed for 5 months + I want to get to work.

A view of the courthouse in downtown St. Paul in the early 1920s

Loafing puts me in this particularly obnoxious and abominable gloom. . . . If it wasn't for Zelda I think I'd disappear for three years. Ship as a sailor or something . . . I'm sick of the flabby semi-intellectual softness in which I flounder with my generation."

Yet Scott continued to welcome friends—old and new—to the cottage. Daytime visits often stretched into the night. Scott's friends made the ten-mile trip from St. Paul to White Bear "to warm themselves in the warm rays thrown off by [Fitzgerald's] glory." But the good times quickly ended in October when the pipes froze in the cottage, prompting the Fitzgeralds to move into the St. Paul Hotel for a brief stay before moving on to the Commodore Hotel, located in Scott's old neighborhood.

Fitzgerald rented an office in St. Paul where he wrote more stories for the *Saturday Evening Post* and continued to revise *The Beautiful and Damned*. While he focused on his writing, Zelda tried to plan for the baby's arrival. Scott noted in his *Ledger* that she was "helpless" in making preparations, purchasing supplies, and finding nursing care. Zelda's friend Xandra Kalman helped her with the necessary arrangements for the coming event. She even arranged for the Fitzgeralds to move into her mother-in-law's house on Goodrich Avenue (named after Xandra's grandfather, Judge Aaron Goodrich).

The Goodrich house provided the space Scott and Zelda needed for the new baby, a full-time nurse, and other household help. Neighbors were thrilled to have the celebrated author in their midst, and Scott always had a friendly greeting for passersby—especially the children. "He was a delightful person," neighbor Ruth Blake recalled. "He used to come out on the step and sit with us, and we kids all held him in awe."

The Fitzgeralds, photographed one month before their daughter, Scottie, was born

Frances Scott Key Fitzgerald (Scottie), pictured here with her mother, was the Fitzgeralds' only child.

On October 26, 1921, Frances Scott Key Fitzgerald (Scottie) was born at the Miller Hospital in St. Paul. Like all other Fitzgerald events, Scottie's birth was proudly hailed in the press: "F. Scott Fitzgerald Is Father of Baby Girl."

In the meantime, Scott wrote a short story titled "The Curious Case of Benjamin Button," which traces the life of a man who is born old and grows up to become an infant. The story was published in *Collier's* magazine. He also revised his play *The Vegetable* and wrote a musical comedy called *Flappers at Midnight.* His novel *The Beautiful and Damned* was published on March 4, 1922.

"Winter Dreams," one of Fitzgerald's most famous short stories, was also published that year. In it he recalled the idyllic summer evenings at White Bear Lake, Minnesota:

> There was a fish jumping and a star shining and the lights around the lake were gleaming. Over on a dark peninsula a piano was playing the songs of last summer and of summers before that . . . and because the sound of a piano over a stretch of water had always seemed beautiful to Dexter he lay perfectly quiet and listened.

The Vegetable was a satire on Americans' lust for success. In the play, a drunken railroad employee becomes president of the United States but eventually finds happiness as a mail carrier. "I do not know of any dialogue by an American which is lighter, more graceful or witty," Edmund Wilson wrote. Although Wilson called Fitzgerald a "dazzling extemporizer," the prominent critic believed the author had yet to write something "more durable." In reviewing *The Beautiful and Damned*, Wilson compared the author to someone who had been given a jewel but didn't know what to do with it. To Wilson, it seemed Fitzgerald was like a brilliant sun whose rays only occasionally reached the earth. Fitzgerald accepted Wilson's criticism and even called it "superb . . . It's the first time I've been done *at length* by an intelligent and sophisticated man and I appreciate it—jeers and all."

The Fitzgerald family moved from city to city during Scottie's early years.

SEVEN

Holding On to the Dream

It was nothing like spending money that ever worried their mind. If they didn't have it, somebody else would have it and spend it for them—they didn't care.

—Jelly Roll Morton

A sense of doom permeates *The Beautiful and Damned.* Scott later told his daughter, "I naturally used many circumstantial events of our early married life. However the emphases were entirely different. We had a much better time than Anthony and Gloria." At the same time, he explained the importance of grasping "the wise and tragic sense of life." He believed that the satisfaction one gets from struggle—not fleeting moments of pleasure—gives life meaning. For Fitzgerald the search for the goal—the dream about it—gave more pleasure than reaching the goal itself.

The *New York Tribune* asked Zelda to review *The Beautiful and Damned*. She wrote under her maiden name, and in the piece she implied that her husband might have used a bit of her own writing in the book. She also wrote an essay for the *Metropolitan Magazine* titled "Eulogy on the Flapper." Scott respected Zelda's talent, often asked for her opinion of his writing, and listened to her advice.

When the summer of 1922 arrived, the Fitzgeralds returned to White Bear Lake and stayed at the White Bear Yacht Club. There, Scott wrote a second book of stories called *Tales of the Jazz Age*. Though sales of his second novel were

The Fitzgeralds spent the summer of 1922 at the White Bear Yacht Club.

The Commodore Hotel in St. Paul served as a haven for the Fitzgeralds and allowed them to indulge in their wild lifestyle.

disappointing, he thought about writing a third one. "I may start my novel and I may not," he wrote to Max Perkins. Roots of *The Great Gatsby* were beginning to form, but at the yacht club on beautiful White Bear Lake, old friends and new poured in to greet its celebrated summer resident. Among Scott's guests was Nobel Prize-winning author Sinclair Lewis, another Minnesotan, though the two never became good friends.

The press continued to court Fitzgerald wherever he went. Finally, the glare of the spotlight, the heavy drinking and noisy parties made life so miserable for other residents at the yacht club that Scott and Zelda were asked to leave. As in the past, they returned to the Commodore Hotel in St. Paul. They felt at home at the Commodore, where they enjoyed elegant tea dances in the afternoon and dined and danced in the rooftop garden at night.

THE JAZZ AGE

When World War I ended in 1918, Americans were in the mood to celebrate. By 1920 U.S. businesses boomed, workers' wages increased, and their working hours shortened. People had more time and money to spend on entertainment and material goods. Henry Ford made cars an affordable item and a symbol of freedom in the country.

The invention of radio brought news, sports, theater, and jazz—the new music of the times—into American homes. Modern advertising methods lured people to buy new things, ranging from vacuum cleaners to baked bread.

For the first time in U.S. history, women were granted the right to vote. They enjoyed other new freedoms too. Many women cut their hair, shortened their skirts, and danced the Charleston, the spirited dance of the day. They became living examples of F. Scott Fitzgerald's "flappers." Society exuded a live-it-up-now aura, and the exuberant middle class emanated hope and excitement.

The music of Jelly Roll Morton, Louis Armstrong, Benny Goodman, Pee Wee Russell, Gene Krupa, Muggsy Spanier, Bix Beiderbecke, and others who introduced the syncopated, inventive rhythms of jazz music invited everyone to join the postwar celebration. In New York, midnight dips in public fountains and riding on top of taxi cabs were part of the "anything goes" spirit of the times.

In her poem "Figs and Thistles," Edna St. Vincent Millay summed up the Jazz Age:

> My candle burns at both ends;
> It will not last the night;
> But, ah, my foes, and, oh, my friends—
> It gives a lovely light.

In his novels and stories, F. Scott Fitzgerald captured both the "lovely light" of the times and the inevitable darkness that followed.

Customers enjoy a speakeasy, a place where alcoholic beverages were sold during Prohibition (the period from 1920 to 1933 when the sale and consumption of alcohol was illegal in the United States). The Fitzgeralds attended speakeasies while living in New York City during the 1920s.

The Fitzgeralds soon grew bored in St. Paul and decided to move back to New York. In September 1922, Scott, Zelda, and Scottie moved to Great Neck, Long Island, about an hour outside of New York City. There Scott hoped to find the peace and quiet he needed to write.

Fitzgerald found America's rush to make money (and spend it) everywhere in New York—from the flashy cars that sped through the night to the glittering partygoers. People danced the Charleston, and the music of Jelly Roll Morton's jazz band, the Red Hot Peppers, filled the air. Scott and Zelda were at the center of it all.

Fitzgerald and young Scottie stroll through Central Park.

Although Scott earned almost $29,000 in 1923—a relatively large income at the time—his expenses far exceeded his income. He hired two people to manage the house, a full-time nurse for Scottie and a part-time laundress. The struggle to maintain their extravagant lifestyle took its toll on his marriage too. Excessive drinking prompted fights and hurt feelings. Disorder and quarrels were almost constant. When the Atlantic City production of *The Vegetable* flopped, Scott had to write more stories to make up for the financial loss. Exhausted and suffering from a chronic cough from smoking, he knew it was time to get away—even if he had to borrow money from his publisher to do it. Scott and Zelda decided to move to France, where they could live on much less money. The colorful literary community in Paris lured them as well.

Edmund Wilson had suggested that Scott look up a promising American author named Ernest Hemingway, who was living in Paris. Scott and Zelda moved into a rented home, the Villa Marie, near St. Raphael, France, on the French Riviera, in the south of France. Scott became familiar with Hemingway's writing. *Three Stories and Ten Poems*, Hemingway's first published work, appeared in 1923. Scott advised Max Perkins to show Hemingway's work to Scribner's. "He's the real thing," Scott wrote to Perkins, but it was Fitzgerald's work that Perkins was anxious to see. In a letter from St. Raphael, Scott reassured him that his novel was under way.

The Fitzgerald family moved from New York to France in 1923, both to save money on living costs and to join the thriving artistic community centered in Paris, above.

Scott, Zelda, and Scottie relax on a summer day in the early 1920s.

> I spent [over two years] uselessly, neither in study nor
> in contemplation but only in drinking and raising hell
> generally. . . . What I'm trying to say is just that I'll
> have to ask you to have patience about the book and
> trust me that . . . for the 1st time in years I'm doing the
> best I can.

He wrote to his St. Paul friend Thomas Boyd, "Well, I shall write a novel better than any novel ever written in America and become par excellence the best second-rater in the world." While Scott worked on *The Great Gatsby*, Zelda developed a romantic friendship with French aviator Edouard Jozan, who flirted with her on the beach. Although the relationship was short lived, it damaged the bond between Scott and Zelda. As he wrote in his *Notebooks* (a personal journal), "That September 1924, I knew something had happened that could never be repaired."

While in France, Fitzgerald began work on what was to become his most famous and widely read book, The Great Gatsby.

EIGHT

Savoring Success

*You said that you would write about these
people; about the very rich. . . . and for once it
would be written by someone who knew what he
was writing of.*

—Ernest Hemingway

To many who knew him, Fitzgerald's drinking seemed a habit impossible to break, but while writing *The Great Gatsby* he stayed sober. On receipt of the manuscript, Max Perkins wrote, "It's magnificent!" And the praise continued: "I think you have every kind of right to be proud of this book. It is an extraordinary book."

Encouraged and hopeful, the Fitzgeralds traveled to Rome and Capri in Italy. While in Rome, Scott reviewed the edited copy of *Gatsby*. When the book was published on April 10, 1925, the critics raved. Gilbert Seldes, a leading literary critic, summed up the favorable response: "Fitzgerald has more than matured; he has mastered his talents and gone soaring in a beautiful flight, leaving behind him . . . all the men of his own generation and most of his elders."

In *Gatsby*, Fitzgerald defined the attraction and failure of the American dream. *"Gatsby,"* wrote Matthew Bruccoli, "becomes the archetypal figure who betrays and is betrayed by the promise of America. By using a narrator (Nick Carraway), Fitzgerald was able to stand both inside and outside of his characters' lives—a distinguishing feature of the novel." But the beauty of the writing is what makes *Gatsby* great. In this passage, Nick describes his neighbor Gatsby's parties:

> There was music from my neighbor's house through the summer nights. In his blue gardens men and girls came and went like moths among the whisperings and the champagne and the stars. At high tide in the afternoon I watched his guests diving from the tower of his raft or taking the sun on the hot sand of his beach while his two motor boats slit the waters of the Sound, drawing aquaplanes over cataracts of foam. On week-ends his Rolls-Royce became an omnibus, bearing parties to and from the city, between nine in the morning and long past midnight, while his station wagon scampered like a brisk yellow bug to meet all trains. And on Mondays, eight servants including an extra gardener toiled all day with mops and scrubbing-brushes and hammers and garden shears, repairing the ravages of the night before.

Initial sales of *The Great Gatsby* were disappointing. But high praise from critics enhanced Fitzgerald's reputation.

While in Italy, the Fitzgerald's marriage seemed to be on the mend. He wrote to his friend John Peale Bishop, "Zelda and I sometimes indulge in terrible four-day rows that always start with a drinking party but we're still enormously in love and about the only truly happily married couple I know."

In May, Scott and Zelda returned to France and moved into an apartment near the Arc de Triomphe in Paris. They

After travelling in Italy, the Fitzgeralds took up residence in a walk-up apartment on the Right Bank at 14 rue de Tilsitt near the famous Arc de Triomphe, above, in Paris.

met Gerald and Sara Murphy, wealthy Americans who had settled in France, and they soon became close friends. The Fitzgeralds had known Gerald's sister Esther in Great Neck, Long Island, and felt a certain kinship with Gerald and Sara even before they met. The Murphys represented the "rich at their best . . . when leisure was combined with charm and culture."

Fitzgerald also met Ernest Hemingway in Paris. The legendary friendship between the two authors began in May 1925. Fitzgerald was twenty-eight, and Hemingway was twenty-five. The friendship had many roots—admiration, rivalry, a love of liquor, and a spirit of adventure.

THE LOST GENERATION

The term *Lost Generation* is used to define a group of American writers who lived and gained prominence in Europe during the 1920s. The group gathered around novelist and critic Gertrude Stein, who reportedly coined the term. The group included F. Scott Fitzgerald, Ernest Hemingway, Ezra Pound, Archibald MacLeish, John Dos Passos, Thornton Wilder, and Hart Crane.

Members of the Lost Generation espoused the unconventional art scene in Paris and exuded a philosophic pessimism in their work. Many of these writers reflected the search for something to believe in after the vast destruction caused by World War I. They tended to reject the conventional literary techniques of the past and the crass materialism that followed the war. They made significant contributions to many of the basic themes and styles of modern literature.

Sylvia Beach, left, owner of *Shakespeare and Company*, the first American lending library and bookshop in Paris, stands with novelist James Joyce, right. *Beach's shop was a favorite meeting place for members of the Lost Generation including Joyce, Hemingway, and Fitzgerald, and can still be visited.*

Ernest Hemingway, right, *met Fitzgerald in May 1925 in the Dingo Bar, rue Delambre, Paris, just after the publication of Fitzgerald's* The Great Gatsby *and shortly before the publication of Hemingway's* The Sun Also Rises.

However, the contrasts between the two men were stark, as biographer Scott Donaldson has noted: "Over six feet tall, a sturdy 190 pounds, and darkly handsome, [Hemingway] formed a striking contrast to the slightly built, blond Fitzgerald. Hemingway had a remarkable gift for inspiring (and later breaking off) male friendships. Fitzgerald, by way of contrast, was particularly inept at developing relationships with male companions. His tendency was to make heroes out of them, often to the discomfort of both parties."

Hemingway appeared strong and courageous, and he moved like an athlete. Fitzgerald admired him immensely. But to Zelda, Hemingway was a phony—"a professional he-man. . .

a pansy with hair on his chest." Hemingway didn't like Zelda either. He believed Zelda aided and abetted Scott's drinking and was therefore thwarting his career.

Hemingway introduced Scott to the literary community that was thriving in Paris in the 1920s. Through Hemingway, Fitzgerald met Gertrude Stein, an American writer and critic, and her companion Alice B. Toklas. Steins's nurturing of artists and writers became legendary. Artists Pablo Picasso and Georges Braque, novelist John Dos Passos, poet,

John Dos Passos, far left, *and Ernest Hemingway,* far right, *were both part of the Lost Generation.*

dramatist, and critic Archibald MacLeish, Hemingway, and Fitzgerald were part of the flock that paid homage to Stein. She was their guru, and a word of praise from her meant a great deal. *The Great Gatsby*, she told Fitzgerald, was "a good book." Fitzgerald was elated.

In the fall of 1925, Scott and Zelda vacationed in Cap d'Antibes on the French Riviera, where the Murphys had a summer home. Like Gertrude Stein, the Murphys attracted some of the most illustrious artists and writers to their home in Antibes. Everyone seemed to blossom in the presence of the Murphys, and they inspired qualities found in some of Fitzgerald's most memorable fictional characters. Like Daisy Buchanan in *Gatsby*, Sara spoke in a voice "full of money." Fitzgerald seemed spellbound by the Murphys almost instantly, and as Scott Donaldson explains, would too often try to emulate them:

> Scott had a severe crush on both Sara and Gerald.... In every social situation, Gerald instinctively understood how to act, how to put others at ease. The word for it was "charm," and at his best Scott could rival Gerald in his capacity to charm other people, mainly women. But he did not like himself when he was expending so much energy simply to please others. Often he would destroy the illusion with an insulting act or remark—and next day, on awaking, try desperately to right the wrong.

While in France, Fitzgerald had planned to work on his novel *Tender Is the Night*, but he spent most the time partying and enjoying *Gatsby*'s critical success. His smoker's cough worsened, and Zelda suffered from stomach pains and other ailments. Arguments erupted between them, and under the influence of alcohol, both exhibited bizarre behavior.

Gertrude Stein was among the first to cultivate the experimental styles of artists of her generation.

Fitzgerald's health deteriorated in 1925, and both he and Zelda began behaving erratically.

For example, on one occasion Scott jumped off a high cliff into the sea, shocking everyone in sight—as he had done years before when he had jumped from a porch roof, astonishing his sister and her friend below. In his *Ledger,* Scott summarized the past year in Europe: "Futile, shameful . . . health gone."

In 1926 the Fitzgeralds returned to the United States. Back home Scott tried to find a peaceful place where he could work on his novel—without the lure of New York nearby.

The Fitzgeralds did their best to appear normal and happy, but both adults were experiencing emotional instability.

NINE

Breakdown

The Fitzgeralds spent Christmas in Montgomery, Alabama, with Zelda's family. Soon after their arrival there, the film studio United Artists asked Scott to write a script for a Hollywood movie. Having saved no money in Europe, Scott viewed the job as a quick and easy source of income. They left Scottie with Scott's parents, who had moved to Washington, D.C., and moved to California

Though Scott received a $3,500 advance payment for the script, he and Zelda quickly spent the money on their social life. He knew he would receive an additional $12,500 when the completed script was accepted. Assuming that final payment would come soon, Scott and Zelda joined the Hollywood party scene. This time Scott was the one found flirting with someone—a young actress named Lois Moran. Zelda became enraged over the innocent relationship. The movie studio rejected Scott's script, so he did not receive the final payment, but Zelda was glad to board a train back home. On their way back, the couple argued about the young actress, and Zelda threw the platinum-and-diamond watch Scott had given her years before out the train window.

Zelda began to develop serious mood swings, and arguments between the couple increased. Both Scott and Zelda hoped that once they settled down in a tranquil place, their married life might improve.

Through John Biggs, Scott's former Princeton roommate, they rented a mansion in Wilmington, Delaware, on the Delaware River. The thirty-two-room house was called Ellerslie. Needing money to pay for the upkeep of the mansion, Scott wrote stories for the *Saturday Evening Post* and for *College Humor.*

Zelda began her own creative activities. She sold several articles to leading magazines and started taking ballet lessons. But neither Scott nor Zelda could resist an occasional trip to New York for a round of parties with old friends. In his *Ledger,* Scott summed up the year 1927 writing, "Total loss at beginning. A lot of fun. Work begins again." And he needed to do much work on his novel *Tender Is the Night.*

In April, distracted by friends and parties, the restless couple decided to spend the summer of 1928 in Paris, where the environment, they thought, would be more conducive to writing. Scott's feelings about France had changed since his earlier visits there. Now, at the age of thirty, he said he missed that "intelligent country." "France," he claimed, "has the only two things toward which we drift as we grow older—intelligence and good manners."

While in Paris, Zelda studied ballet with Lubov Egorova, a former Russian ballerina. Zelda became completely involved with dance lessons—a preoccupation that left little time for Scott. She also worked on her writing and used any income from it to continue her ballet lessons. At the same time, her behavior showed troublesome signs. In conversation she became silent for long periods of time and then suddenly

To escape the distractions of life on the East Coast, Fitzgerald returned to Paris, right, *in 1928 to work on* Tender Is the Night.

made incoherent statements. Yet, according to Matthew Bruccoli, her writing displayed a "lush style and sensitivity to the moods of time and place."

For Scott, highlights of that summer included meeting the esteemed writer James Joyce. Fitzgerald wrote to Max Perkins that Joyce had come to dinner and talked about finishing his novel *Finnegan's Wake* in three or four years, but that "mine will be done *sure* in September." Max Perkins had heard such optimistic reports before and urged him to work harder. By the end of the summer, Scott had finished only two chapters, and in October the Fitzgeralds returned to America.

Back home at Ellerslie, Scott had to write—and sell—more short stories to keep up with household expenses. He had borrowed money against future sales of *Tender Is the Night*, but the book was still unfinished. Zelda became more and more involved with the world of dance. Dancing had become an obsession. When their lease on Ellerslie ended in the spring of 1929, both Scott and Zelda had to concentrate on yet another move. Once again they decided to return to Europe. Scott assured Max Perkins that he would revise the third and fourth chapters of his novel on the boat, but he failed to do so.

They spent the summer of 1929 in Cannes, on the French Riviera. "I am working night + day on novel from new angle that I think will solve previous difficulties," Scott wrote to Perkins. Meanwhile, Zelda continued her intensive ballet work with increasing strain.

Hemingway's second novel, *A Farewell to Arms*, (a tragic love story set in World War I Italy), had become a big success, and Fitzgerald was inspired to finish his own novel. When Fitzgerald heard that Gertrude Stein had called him (Fitzgerald) "the most talented writer of his generation, the one with the brightest flame," he became upset. He felt that her praise was a slight to Hemingway, but Hemingway assured Fitzgerald that he felt no competition with him. He told Scott that "there can be no such thing between serious writers—They are all in the same boat . . . . You're on the boat but you're getting touchy because you haven't finished your novel—that's all—I understand it."

Scott dashed off stories for the *Saturday Evening Post* to pay his family's bills. He must have found it difficult to focus on his novel as Zelda's obsession with dance began to indicate signs of mental illness. At a flower market, she told Scott that the flowers were talking to her. She grew angry when others failed to hear the voices she was hearing. In April 1930, "in an acute state of anxiety," Zelda was admitted to Malmaison clinic near Paris for psychiatric help.

Zelda's breakdown, the breakdown of the Fitzgeralds' marriage, and their mounting money problems mirrored the Great Depression in America in the early 1930s. At that time, the U.S. economy plunged, banks closed, and people lost their jobs as companies went bankrupt. Fitzgerald's writing about "the beautiful people" and their eat-drink-and-be-merry attitude no longer fit the times.

The Great Depression left many people unemployed and destitute. They spent hours standing in "breadlines" to get free food.

Scott had not invested money in the stock market, so he didn't suffer the financial losses that many others did. But because of Zelda's illness and the ongoing cost of treatment, he had to scramble to meet his overwhelming expenses. Despite her illness, Zelda continued writing and also began painting, which Scott encouraged. She liked to paint ballet scenes and cityscapes of New York and Paris. Scott arranged exhibitions of her work in Paris and New York.

On May 11, Zelda discharged herself from Malmaison against the advice of her doctor. Soon afterward she suffered hallucinations resulting in a suicide attempt. She was then admitted to Valmont clinic in Glion, Switzerland, where consulting psychiatrist Dr. Oscar Forel diagnosed Zelda as schizophrenic, a psychotic disorder characterized by a loss of contact with the real environment. The illness causes disordered thoughts and feelings that often result in hallucinations and delusions. Zelda entered Dr. Forel's Les Rives de Prangins clinic near Geneva, Switzerland, for treatment.

During Zelda's treatment, Scottie stayed with her governess, Mademoiselle Sereze, in the Fitzgeralds' Paris apartment and attended the Cours Dieterlin school there. She learned to speak French, which delighted her parents. Scottie loved to dress up for almost any occasion and enjoyed being in the limelight. She made friends easily and showed great curiosity about people.

While in Switzerland, Fitzgerald learned that his father had died on January 26, 1931, in Washington, D.C. Although they had grown apart over the years, Scott was always grateful to his father for having praised his early writings at St. Paul Academy. Scott attended the funeral in Washington and returned to Europe at the end of February.

Many aspects of Zelda's life influenced her choice of subject matter in her paintings. She painted one series based on children's fairy tales. The self-portrait above is from a series of works featuring herself and her husband.

Scottie enjoyed dressing up and travelling with her parents.

After Zelda's discharge from the Prangins clinic in September 1931, the family returned permanently to the United States. The Fitzgeralds visited Zelda's parents in Montgomery and rented a house there. Zelda needed a quiet place, and she wanted to be near her parents because of Judge Sayre's failing health. In November 1931, Metro-Goldwyn-Mayer asked Scott to come to Hollywood to write a screenplay. Needing the money, he accepted the offer. He finished the work in five weeks and returned to Montgomery and, he hoped, to a period of rest.

In January Zelda suffered severe asthma attacks, and Scott decided to take her to Florida to get away from the dampness in Montgomery. While there, he wrote to Max Perkins, "At last I am going to spend five consecutive months on my novel . . . adding 41,000 new words." He also told Perkins that the manuscript would be ready for publication at the end of that period. Fitzgerald's promises and good intentions were nothing new to Perkins, but this time he sensed a fresh resolve in Scott's words and hoped he was right.

Despite his personal troubles, Fitzgerald maintained a close relationship with his daughter, Scottie, who enjoyed posing for the camera.

TEN

Dear Scottie...

For sweetest things turn sourest by their deeds;
Lilies that fester smell far worse than weeds.
—William Shakespeare

On the way back from Florida to Montgomery, Zelda became obsessed with irrational fears. One night she drank Scott's flask of liquor, increasing her anxiety and confusion. She insisted on being hospitalized, and on February 12, 1932, she was admitted to the Henry Phipps Psychiatric Clinic of the Johns Hopkins University Hospital in Baltimore, Maryland, where she was evaluated and then received full-time care.

During Zelda's stay at Phipps, she worked on her novel *Save Me the Waltz*. When it was finished the following month, she sent it to Max Perkins who accepted it for publication. But Scott's reaction was not supportive. He insisted that Zelda had taken material from his novel for her own. After making careful revisions, however, Scott reported to Perkins that "Zelda's novel is now good, improved in every way."

95

While in Baltimore, Fitzgerald met poet T. S. Eliot, left.

    While Zelda remained at Phipps, Scott and eleven-year-old Scottie rented a fifteen-room house outside Baltimore, not far from the Henry Phipps Clinic. The house was named La Paix (Peace), and Scott and Scottie enjoyed many peaceful hours together there. He enjoyed reading Charles Dickens's *Great Expectations* to her and teaching her to play chess.

    To relieve his loneliness, Scott often joined in games and skits with Scottie and her friends Eleanor, Frances, and Andrew Turnbull, children of the Fitzgeralds' friends Margaret and Bayard Turnbull. The Turnbulls were not close friends of Scott and Zelda, but through the Turnbulls, Scott met the renowned poet T. S. Eliot. Scott called him "the greatest living poet," and Eliot praised Fitzgerald's *Gatsby.*

    Visitors—young and old alike—relieved Scott's loneliness

at La Paix during Zelda's absence. When Mollie Fitzgerald visited her son, she always brought him candy in hopes of luring him away from alcohol, which by that time he was drinking regularly. Scott's life centered entirely around Zelda, Scottie, and close friends.

Although Zelda had not been cured at Phipps (modern medications that can control schizophrenic behavior were not yet in use), she was able to return to La Paix in June and to continue periodic outpatient treatment. To pay the increasing bills, Scott wrote more short stories for the *Saturday Evening Post*. His work was interrupted briefly when he was hospitalized for symptoms of typhoid fever, but he even managed to turn that event into a short story titled "One Interne." His stay at Johns Hopkins University Hospital marked the beginning of periodic hospital visits for alcoholism and recurring tuberculosis. Still, he continued to drink and smoke.

Both Scott and Zelda spent time at Johns Hopkins University Hospital, above, *to receive treatment for physical and psychological problems.*

Zelda's novel *Save Me the Waltz* was published on October 7, 1932. An autobiographical story, it included her early family relationships and her marriage to Scott. Max Perkins had hoped that the book would help pay off Scott's debts—especially his debt to Scribner's, which had advanced him so much money on his unfinished novel. But *Waltz* did not receive good reviews, and it failed to sell.

Drinking and the need to write short stories for cash continued to delay Fitzgerald's novel. As he worried about Zelda, he drank more and slept less. The bright spot in his life continued to be Scottie. Even when she was away at summer camp, he stayed in close touch through letters, especially when Zelda became less and less able to do so. He was concerned that having been raised in mansions, waited on by servants, and treated to trips to Europe all before the age of twelve, Scottie might become lazy. He worried that she might grow up "soft" and "cynical" and not develop her potential. On August 8, 1933, while Scottie was at camp, he wrote to her:

> All I believe in in life is the rewards for virtue (according to your talents) and the punishments for not fulfilling your duties, which are doubly costly. If there is such a volume in the camp library, will you ask Mrs. Tyson to let you look up a sonnet of Shakespeare's in which the line occurs "Lilies that fester smell far worse than weeds." . . .
>
> Things to think about: What am I really aiming at? How good am I really in comparison to my contemporaries in regard to:
>
> a) Scholarship
> b) Do I really understand about people and am I able to get along with them?
> c) Am I trying to make my body a useful instrument or am I neglecting it?

At the same time, Max Perkins was concerned about Fitzgerald's lack of progress with his own talents. He wrote to Scott:

> Whenever any of these new writers come up who are brilliant, I always realize that you have more talent and more skill than any of them; but circumstances have prevented you from realizing upon the fact for a long time.

Finally, on April 12, 1934, *Tender Is the Night* was published. It received mixed reviews. Among the best was one by Gilbert Seldes, "who thought the novel so intense that he had to put it down in order to stop to think and to feel." The book was not a big money maker as the publisher had hoped. Its topic—rich Americans living on the French Riviera—was out of step with the tough economic times in America. Considering the circumstances, the book sold reasonably well. When Gertrude Stein told Scott that she "liked a lot" of the book, he was pleased to receive praise from the renowned literary guru.

Though *Tender Is the Night* was "undervalued in its own time," according to Scott Donaldson, "it has grown in rank with *Gatsby* as the work on which Fitzgerald's critical reputation most securely rests." Like *Gatsby*, it serves as a fitting epitaph to an era of Jazz Age parties. The book is a beautifully written account of the general decline of a few glamorous Americans in Europe.

The critical success of Fitzgerald's novel coincided with Zelda's deteriorating condition. She had been readmitted to Phipps, where she made no improvement. She then moved to Craig House, a sanatorium in Beacon, New York, and finally back to Baltimore, Maryland, where she entered the Sheppard and Enoch Pratt Hospital.

The French Riviera, a region where the Fitzgeralds had lived on and off for years, was the setting for Tender Is the Night.

Zelda attempted suicide many times while in the hospital, and there seemed to be no chance of recovery. Scott realized that their life together was over, and his heartache can be felt in one particular sentence found in his *Notebooks*: "I left my capacity for hoping on the little roads that led to Zelda's sanitarium." One month after her admission to the hospital, Zelda wrote to Scott, "I love you anyway—even if there isn't any me or any love or even any life."

Fitzgerald continued to write during the mid-1930s, despite failing health.

ELEVEN

The Twilight's Last Gleaming

Toward the end of 1934, Fitzgerald compiled a collection of his short stories called *Taps at Reveille*. The volume was published in 1935 and received good reviews. Despite bouts with tuberculosis, Scott continued to write and sold stories to the *Saturday Evening Post*, *McCall's*, and *Liberty* magazines. Debts, however, loomed ever larger. Scottie's boarding school tuition combined with worry over Zelda caused Scott's physical and emotional health to suffer. He drank more, and the more he drank, the more depressed he became. It was not easy to act on his own philosophy—that one should "be able to see that things are hopeless and yet be determined to make them otherwise," as he wrote in "The Crack-Up."

In "The Crack-Up" Fitzgerald wrote:

> I saw that for a long time I had not liked people and things, but only followed the rickety old pretense of liking. I saw that even my love for those closest to me was becoming only an attempt to love, that my casual relations . . . were only what I remembered I should do, from other days. . . . I became bitter about such things as the sound of the radio, the advertisements in the magazines, the screech of tracks, the dead silence of the country—contemptuous of human softness . . . hating the night when I couldn't sleep and hating the day because it went toward night.

Fitzgerald wrote "The Crack-Up" for *Esquire* magazine. He could not write love stories in such a dark mood so he wrote about his depression—the only topic he could write about at that time. That essay and the two that followed it ("Pasting It Together" and "Handle with Care") became his best-known and most widely read essays. At that time, popular authors did not display their emotional problems openly and honestly in print, however, so the pieces shocked readers. By writing about his breakdown without disguising it in a fictional character, Fitzgerald risked his reputation as a successful literary writer. John Dos Passos rebuked him for wasting his talent. Ernest Hemingway viewed the articles as "shameful" and "cowardly."

Writing "The Crack-Up" series helped Fitzgerald cope with his depression, and publication of the essays helped to reduce his debts. But he still owed thousands of dollars to his friends—to Harold Ober, his old friend and agent, in particular. Ann and Harold Ober helped Scott in more personal ways too. When Scottie entered the Ethel Walker School in Simsbury, Connecticut, in 1936, she stayed with the Obers in Scarsdale, New York, on holidays, and the Obers became surrogate

parents while she was at school. Theirs was a warm relationship, and both Scott and Zelda were grateful for the loving attention the Obers gave Scottie.

By the spring of 1936, Zelda had made no improvement
at the Sheppard-Pratt Hospital, so she was transferred to
Highland Hospital in Asheville, North Carolina, where new
treatments for mental illness were being used. Once she was
established at Highland, Scott went back to Baltimore to visit
his mother, who was ill. Mollie Fitzgerald died in August 1936
at the age of seventy-six. Scott had broken his shoulder in a
diving accident that summer and could not attend the funeral.
Though his mother had doted on him as a child and showered
him with love, she and Scott lost touch over the years. He
believed he had not been a "good son." "She was a defiant old
woman," he wrote, "defiant in her love for me in spite of my
neglect of her, and it would have been quite within her
character to have died that I may live."

Scott enjoyed writing letters to Scottie. He was determined that she not adopt the lifestyle of the idle rich—many
of whom had daughters at the Ethel Walker School. He did
not want Scottie to emulate her parents' "road to disaster"; he
wanted her to learn from it. In August 1937, he wrote to her:

> I shall somehow manage not to appear in a taxicab on
> Thanksgiving and thus disgrace you before all those
> "nice" girls. Isn't it somewhat old-fashioned to
> describe girls in expensive backgrounds as "nice"? I
> will bet two-thirds of the girls at Miss Walker's School
> have at least one grandparent that peddled old leather
> in the slums of New York, Chicago, or London, and if
> I thought you were accepting the standards of the
> cosmopolitan rich, I would much rather have you in a
> Southern school, where . . . the word "nice" is not
> debased to such a ludicrous extent. I have seen the

whole racket, and if there is any more disastrous road than that from Park Avenue to the Rue de la Paix and back again, I don't know it.

Although Scott had inherited enough money from his mother to relieve some of his financial burden, he was quickly overdrawn at the bank and discouraged by the rejection of his new stories. His reputation as an alcoholic—fueled by "The Crack-Up" essays—was well established by 1937, and his chances of seeing more of his stories in print were slim. Once again, Fitzgerald returned to Hollywood where Metro-Goldwyn-Mayer offered him a job as a screenwriter. It seemed to be his last hope.

For a great writer like Fitzgerald, "going Hollywood" meant lowering his standards. Others would rewrite his scripts, and his only screen credit was for *Three Comrades* in 1938. During those Hollywood years of 1937–1940, however, he did begin his fourth—and he hoped his best—novel, *The Last Tycoon*. The story was based on the life of Irving Thalberg, the Metro-Goldwyn-Mayer studio head. The main female character was inspired by Sheilah Graham, a well-known movie columnist in Hollywood.

Fitzgerald first saw Sheilah Graham at a party given by Robert Benchley, a popular humorist, actor, and critic. Scott was struck by Sheilah's resemblance to Zelda, and echoes of that moment come through in *The Last Tycoon*: "Across the four feet of moonlight, the eyes he knew looked back at him, a curl blew a little on a familiar forehead; the lips parted—the same. An awful fear went over him, and he wanted to cry aloud."

They met again at other parties and soon fell in love. Scott's drinking ignited fights between them, but when he was

Fitzgerald became romantically involved with columnist Sheilah Graham during his time in Hollywood.

sober they enjoyed concerts, visits to art museums, and dinner parties with friends. Although Scott had shown little interest in politics throughout his life, he began to embrace the causes that concerned his liberal friends in the Screen Writer's Guild—namely opposition to Nazism (the movement led by German dictator Adolf Hitler). In a letter to Scottie during her first year at Vassar College, he warned her about the dangers of identifying with any pro-Nazi students she might meet:

You will notice that there is a strongly organized left-wing movement there. I do not particularly want you to think about politics, but I do not want you to set yourself against this movement. I am known as a left-wing sympathizer and would be proud if you were. In any case, I should feel outraged if you identified yourself with Nazism . . . in any form.

Scott wrote many loving letters to Scottie while she was at Vassar, but their tone was sometimes critical and demanding. She was grateful for his advice about the importance of reading great books, but when he told her what courses to take, what boys to date, and what parties to attend, she thought he went too far.

Fitzgerald's health affected his behavior as well as his writing while living in Hollywood. His life was punctuated by alcoholic binges—even when visiting Zelda in the hospital in North Carolina or with friends in New York. In February 1939, following a weekend of heavy drinking in New York, Scott was hospitalized for a lung infection, and he was in a state of confusion.

Although Scott curtailed his drinking in 1940, heart problems began to plague him. In November he suffered a heart attack in a Hollywood drugstore. Complete bed rest was ordered while recuperating. Because of the noise above his apartment, he moved into Sheilah Graham's quiet apartment nearby and worked on his novel, which by then was more than half finished. According to his plan, he expected to have the work completed by January 15, 1941. On December 21, 1940, Fitzgerald suffered another heart attack and died in Graham's apartment. He was forty-four years old.

"Fitzgerald died believing he was a failure," Matthew Bruccoli wrote. "[He should not] have died of neglect in

Hollywood . . . haunting bookstores unrecognized (as he was the last-but-one time I saw him)," fellow writer John O'Hara wrote. But the neglect would not last long. His unfinished novel, *The Last Tycoon*, was published in 1941. In the *Saturday Review of Literature*, the esteemed American author Stephen Vincent Benét praised the book in his memorable tribute to F. Scott Fitzgerald:

> You can take off your hats now, gentlemen, and I think perhaps you had better. This is not a legend, this is a reputation—and, seen in perspective, it may well be one of the most secure reputations of our time.

Fitzgerald, toward the end of his life

Epilogue

Because Fitzgerald had not been a practicing Catholic for many years, he was not allowed to be buried in the Fitzgerald family plot in Rockville, Maryland. He was buried in Rockville Union Cemetery. Eight years later, Zelda died in a fire at the Highland Hospital, and she was buried next to Scott. In 1975 the remains of both were returned to the Fitzgerald family plot at St. Mary's Church and buried alongside Scott's parents.

Between 1945 and 1950, a revival of Fitzgerald's work swept across the country, and by 1960 the revival had become "a resurrection." He is considered a classic American author. Millions of copies of his books have been sold and continue to sell, and movies of *Tender Is the Night* and *The Great Gatsby* have been made and remade over the years.

The Princeton University library houses the F. Scott Fitzgerald Papers—including the priceless collection of manuscripts, notebooks, photos, scrapbooks, and letters that Scottie donated to the library in 1950. The Fitzgerald collection draws more scholars than any other at the library.

In St. Paul, Minnesota, a life-size bronze statue of Fitzgerald stands in Rice Park—only a few minutes away from the Summit Avenue neighborhood where he grew up. In 1994 the city's historic World Theater was renamed the Fitzgerald Theater in his honor. And at his former school, St. Paul Academy, students are talking about, reading about, and writing about F. Scott Fitzgerald year after year. It would be difficult to find anything that would have pleased him more than that.

Timeline

1853 Birth of Edward Fitzgerald at Glenmary farm near Rockville, Maryland

1858 Birth of Anthony D. Sayre in Tuskegee, Alabama

1860 Birth of Mary (Mollie) McQuillan in St. Paul, Minnesota; birth of Minnie Buckner Machen in Eddyville, Kentucky

1884 Marriage of Anthony Sayre and Minnie Machen in June

1890 Marriage of Edward Fitzgerald and Mollie McQuillan in February

1896 Birth of Francis Scott Key Fitzgerald in St. Paul, Minnesota, on September 24

1898 Edward Fitzgerald's furniture company fails; takes job with Procter & Gamble in Buffalo, New York

1900 Birth of Zelda Sayre in Montgomery, Alabama, on July 24

1901 Fitzgerald family moves to Syracuse, New York, in January; Annabel Fitzgerald born in July

1903 Fitzgerald family moves back to Buffalo in September

1908 Edward Fitzgerald loses his job; family returns to St. Paul; Scott enters St. Paul Academy (SPA)

1909 Judge Sayre is appointed Associate Justice of the Supreme Court of Alabama; publication of "The Mystery of the Raymond Mortgage" in SPA's *Now & Then* (Scott's first appearance in print)

1911 Scott enters the Newman School in Hackensack, New Jersey

1912 Production of *The Captured Shadow* in St. Paul; Scott meets Father Cyril Sigourney Fay and Shane Leslie

1913 Production of *The Coward* in St. Paul; Scott enters Princeton University; meets Edmund Wilson and John Peale Bishop

1914 Production of *Assorted Spirits* in St. Paul; Scott contributes to Princeton *Tiger*; Zelda enters Sidney Lanier High School; production of *Fie! Fie! Fi-Fi!*—one of Scott's first Princeton Triangle Club shows

1915 Scott meets Ginevra King; publication of "Shadow Laurels" in *Nassau Literary Magazine (Nassau Lit.);* production of *The Evil Eye* by Triangle Club

1916 Production of *Safety First* by Triangle Club

1917 Scott receives commission as infantry second lieutenant; reports to Fort Leavenworth, Kansas; begins *The Romantic Egotist*

1918 Reports to Camp Taylor in Louisville, Kentucky; completes first draft of *The Romantic Egotist*; submits novel to Scribner's; transferred to Camp Gordon, Georgia; Zelda graduates from Sidney Lanier High School; Scott reports to Camp Sheridan near Montgomery, Alabama; meets Zelda Sayre; novel rejected; Scott reports to Camp Mills, Long Island, to await embarkation; WWI ends before unit sent overseas; returns to Camp Sheridan

1919 Scott is discharged from army; moves to New York and works for the Barron Collier advertising agency; quits job and returns to St. Paul to rewrite novel; Maxwell Perkins of Scribner's accepts *This Side of Paradise* on September 16; Scott becomes a client of Harold Ober at the Reynolds Agency; sells "Heads and Shoulders" to the *Saturday Evening Post*; visits Zelda in November; November 1919–February 1920, the *Smart Set* publishes "The Debutante," "Porcelain and Pink," "Benediction," and "Dalyrimple Goes Wrong"

1920 The *Saturday Evening Post* publishes "Myra Meets His Family," "The Camel's Back," "Bernice Bobs Her Hair," "The Ice Palace," and "The Offshore Pirate"; *This Side of Paradise* published on March 26; marries Zelda on April 3; the *Smart Set* publishes "May Day" in July; *Flappers and Philosophers*, Scott's first short-story collection, is published on September 10; the Fitzgeralds move to New York City

1921 Fitzgeralds make first trip to Europe; rent house in White Bear Lake; *The Beautiful and Damned* serialized in *Metropolitan Magazine*; Scottie born on October 26; move to St. Paul

1922 Fitzgeralds move to White Bear Yacht Club; *The Beautiful and Damned* published on March 4; the *Smart Set* publishes "The Diamond as Big as the Ritz"; *Tales of the Jazz Age*, Scott's second collection of short stories, published on September 22; move to Great Neck, Long Island; *Metropolitan Magazine* publishes "Winter Dreams"

1923 *The Vegetable* is published on April 27; play fails in Atlantic City, New Jersey

1924 Fitzgeralds sail for France; rent Villa Marie in St. Raphael; "Absolution" published in *American Mercury*; Scott writes *The Great Gatsby*; Zelda has flirtation with French aviator Edouard Jozan; "The Sensible Thing" published in *Liberty*; move to Rome

1925 *The Great Gatsby* is published on April 10; Fitzgeralds move to Paris; Fitzgeralds meet Gerald and Sara Murphy; Scott meets Ernest Hemingway

1926 "The Rich Boy" published in *Redbook* magazine; play version of *The Great Gatsby* produced on Broadway; *All the Sad Young Men*, Scott's third short-story collection, published on February 26; Fitzgeralds return to the Riviera; return to the United States in December

1927 Fitzgeralds go to Hollywood to work on *Lipstick* (unproduced) for United Artists; Scott meets Lois Moran; Fitzgeralds rent Ellerslie in Delaware; Zelda begins ballet lessons

1928 Fitzgeralds return to Paris; "The Scandal Detectives" published in the *Saturday Evening Post*; Zelda begins ballet lessons with Lubov Egorova; return to the United States and Ellerslie; Zelda begins writing short stories

1929 "The Last of the Belles" published in the *Saturday Evening Post*; Fitzgeralds return to Europe

1930 Scott and Zelda travel to North Africa; Zelda has first breakdown, enters Malmaison clinic, then Valmont in Switzerland; "First Blood" published in the *Saturday Evening Post*; first Josephine Perry story published; Zelda enters Prangins clinic; Scott lives in Switzerland; Zelda starts painting

1931 Edward Fitzgerald dies; Scott attends funeral; reports to Sayres about Zelda; "Babylon Revisited" published in the *Saturday Evening Post*; Scott and Zelda spend two weeks in France; Zelda released from Prangins on September 15; Fitzgeralds return to the United States; rent house in Montgomery, Alabama; Scott goes to Hollywood to work on *Red-Headed Woman* for Metro-Goldwyn-Mayer; Judge Sayre dies on November 17

1932 Zelda suffers her second breakdown; enters Phipps Psychiatric Clinic in Baltimore; completes first draft of her novel, *Save Me the Waltz*, while at Phipps; Scott rents La Paix outside Baltimore; Zelda discharged from Phipps on June 26; Zelda's story "A Couple of Nuts" published in *Scribner's Magazine*; *Save Me the Waltz* published on October 7; Zelda's art is exhibited in Baltimore

1933 Zelda's play, *Scandalabra*, produced by the Vagabond Junior Players in Baltimore; Scott rents house in Baltimore

1934 Serialization of *Tender Is the Night* in *Scribner's Magazine*; Zelda has her third breakdown; enters Sheppard-Pratt Hospital; Zelda transferred to Craig House in Beacon, New York; Zelda's art exhibit opens in New York; *Tender Is the Night* published on April 12; Zelda returns to Sheppard-Pratt

1935 Scott moves to the Oak Hall Hotel in Tryon, North Carolina; *Taps at Reveille* is published on March 20; Scott begins writing "The Crack-Up" essays

1936 Zelda enters Highland Hospital in Ashevillle, North Carolina; Scott goes to Grove Park Inn in Asheville; Mollie McQuillan Fitzgerald dies; Scottie enters the Ethel Walker School in Connecticut

1937 Scott stays at the Oak Hall Hotel in Tryon; goes to Hollywood to work for MGM; meets Sheilah Graham; visits Zelda in Asheville; works on scripts for *Three Comrades, Infidelity, Marie Antoinette, The Women,* and *Madame Curie*

1938 Fitzgeralds spend Easter at Virginia Beach, Virginia; Scott rents bungalow at Malibu Beach, California; Scottie enters Vassar College; Scott moves to cottage at Encino, California

1939 Scott works briefly on *Gone with the Wind*; takes freelance jobs at Paramount, Universal, Twentieth Century Fox, MGM, and Columbia Studios; Fitzgeralds travel to Cuba in April; Scott breaks with Harold Ober in July; begins work on *The Last Tycoon*

1940 Publication of "Pat Hobby's Christmas Wish" (the first of a seventeen-story series) in *Esquire* magazine; Zelda discharged from Highland Hospital; moves in with her mother in Montgomery; Scott works on *Cosmopolitan (Babylon Revisited)* script; has a heart attack in November; moves to Sheilah Graham's Hollywood apartment; dies of heart attack on December 21; buried in Rockville Union Cemetery in Rockville, Maryland

1941 *The Last Tycoon* published on October 27

1945 *The Crack-Up* published on August 12 (edited by Edmund Wilson)

1947 Zelda leaves Montgomery to return to Highland Hospital in Asheville, North Carolina

1948 Zelda dies in fire at Highland Hospital on March 10; buried with Scott in Rockville, Maryland

1975 Scott and Zelda are reburied in St. Mary's Cemetery in Rockville

1986 Scottie dies and is buried with her parents

Sources

p. 8   Dave Page and John Koblas, *F. Scott Fitzgerald in Minnesota: Toward the Summit* (St. Cloud, MN: North Star Press of St. Cloud, Inc., 1996), 24.

p. 8   Claudia Pierpont, "For Love and Money," *The New Yorker,* July 3, 2000, 77.

p. 17   Page and Koblas, 23.

p. 19   Scott Donaldson, *Hemingway vs. Fitzgerald: The Rise and Fall of a Literary Friendship* (New York: The Overlook Press, 1999), 17.

p. 21   Page and Koblas, 49.

p. 22   Ibid., 54

pp. 23–24   Ibid., 66.

p. 24   Cleanth Brooks, R. W. B. Lewis, and Robert Penn Warren, *American Literature: The Makers and the Making,* Vol. 11 (New York: St. Martin's Press, 1973), 2282.

p. 27   *F. Scott Fitzgerald: A Life in Letters*, ed. Matthew J. Bruccoli (New York: Simon & Schuster, 1994), xix.

p. 27   Ibid., 480.

p. 29   Page and Koblas, 76.

p. 30   Ibid., 77.

pp. 31–32   Scott Donaldson, *Fool for Love: F. Scott Fitzgerald* (New York: Congdon & Weeds, 1983), 27.

p. 32   Brooks, et al., 2282.

p. 32   Oscar James Campbell, Justine Van Gundy, and Caroline Shrodes, eds., *Patterns for Living* (New York: The Macmillan Publishing Company, 1947), 153.

p. 32   Page and Koblas, 81.

p. 35   Donaldson, *Fool for Love*, 51.

p. 35   Ibid., 35.

p. 37   Ibid., 50.

p. 37   Ibid., 36.

p. 38   Ibid., 60.

p. 40   Bruccoli, *A Life in Letters*, 21.

p. 40   Matthew Bruccoli, *Some Sort of Epic Grandeur: The Life of F. Scott Fitzgerald.* (New York: Harcourt Brace Jovanovich, 1981), 96.

pp. 46–47   Ibid., 114.

pp. 47–48   Ibid., 115.

p. 48   Ibid.

p. 51   Brooks, et al., 2285.

p. 51   Donaldson, *Fool for Love*, 26.

p. 51   F. Scott Fitzgerald, *This Side of Paradise* (New York: Charles Scribner's Sons, 1920), 83.

p. 52   Bruccoli, *A Life in Letters*, 37.

p. 52   Fitzgerald, *This Side of Paradise*, 282.

p. 52   Bruccoli, *Some Sort of Epic Grandeur*, 140.

p. 56   Campbell, et al., 151.

p. 57   Bruccoli, *Some Sort of Epic Grandeur*, 151.

p. 57   Page and Koblas, 109.

p. 57   Ibid., 107.

p. 57   Ibid., 108.

p. 57   Ibid., 107.

pp. 58–59   F. Scott Fitzgerald, *The Short Stories of F. Scott Fitzgerald*, ed. Matthew Bruccoli (New York: Charles Scribner's Sons, 1989), xi.

p. 59–60   Bruccoli, *A Life in Letters*, 48.

p. 60   Page and Koblas, 124.

p. 60   Ibid., 117.

p. 60   Ibid., 126.

p. 62   Ibid., 118.

p. 63   *The Short Stories of F. Scott Fitzgerald*, 223.

p. 63   Donaldson, *Hemingway vs. Fitzgerald*, 281.

p. 63	Ibid.
p. 63	Ibid.
p. 65	Bruccoli, *Some Sort of Epic Grandeur*, 155.
p. 65	Bruccoli, *A Life in Letters*, 465.
p. 67	Page and Koblas, 130.
p. 73	Bruccoli, *A Life in Letters*, 82.
p. 73	Bruccoli, *Some Sort of Epic Grandeur*, 195.
p. 73	Ibid., 197.
p. 73	Ibid., 198.
p. 75	Ibid., 213.
p. 75	Ibid., 221.
p. 76	Ibid., 223.
p. 76	F. Scott Fitzgerald, *The Great Gatsby* (New York: Charles Scribner's Sons, 1925), 43.
p. 76	Bruccoli, *Some Sort of Epic Grandeur*, 211.
p. 77	Ibid., 233.
p. 79	Donaldson, *Hemingway vs. Fitzgerald*, 55.
pp.79–80	Bruccoli, *Some Sort of Epic Grandeur*, 229.
p. 81	Donaldson, *Hemingway vs. Fitzgerald*, 63.
p. 81	Ibid., 87.
p. 81	Ibid., 88.
p. 83	Bruccoli, *Some Sort of Epic Grandeur*, 256.
p. 86	Ibid., 263.
p. 86	Ibid., 257.
p. 87	Ibid., 273.
p. 87	Ibid., 267.
p. 88	Ibid., 284.
p. 88	Ibid., 288.
p. 88	Ibid., 293.
p. 89	Ibid.
p. 93	Ibid., 324.
p. 95	Ibid., 327.
p. 96	Ibid., 345.
p. 98	*The Short Stories of F. Scott Fitzgerald*, 318.
pp. 98–99	*Patterns for Living,* 145.
p. 99	Bruccoli, *Some Sort of Epic Grandeur*, 359.
p. 99	Donaldson, *Hemingway vs. Fitzgerald*, 172.
p. 99	Ibid., 179.
p. 100	Ibid., 170.
p. 101	Bruccoli, *Some Sort of Epic Grandeur*, 366.
p. 101	Bruccoli, *A Life in Letters*, 285.
p. 103	Brooks, et al., 2313.
p. 104	Bruccoli, *Some Sort of Epic Grandeur*, 405.
p. 104	Brooks, et al., 2314.
p. 105	Bruccoli, *Some Sort of Epic Grandeur*, 409.
p.105	Ibid.
p.105	*Patterns for Living,* 147.
pp. 105–106	Bruccoli, *Some Sort of Epic Grandeur*, 411.
p. 106	Ibid., 429.
p. 108	Bruccoli, *A Life in Letters*, 366.
p. 108	Ibid., xxii.
p. 109	Bruccoli, *Some Sort of Epic Grandeur*, 489.
p. 109	Donaldson, *Hemingway vs. Fitzgerald*, 254.
p. 111	Bruccoli, *A Life in Letters*, xxii.

Bibliography

Brooks, Cleanth, R. W. B. Lewis, and Robert Penn Warren. *American Literature: The Makers and the Making.* Vol. 11. New York: St. Martin's Press, 1973.

Bruccoli, Matthew J. *F. Scott Fitzgerald: A Descriptive Bibliography.* Pittsburgh: University of Pittsburgh Press, 1972.

———. *Some Sort of Epic Grandeur: The Life of F. Scott Fitzgerald.* New York: Harcourt Brace Jovanovich, 1981.

———. *Supplement to F. Scott Fitzgerald: A Descriptive Bibliography.* Pittsburgh: University of Pittsburgh Press, 1980.

Campbell, Oscar James, Justine Van Gundy, and Caroline Shrodes, editors. *Patterns for Living.* New York: The Macmillan Publishing Company, 1947.

Cerf, Bennett, editor. *Great Modern Short Stories.* New York: Random House, 1942.

Donaldson, Scott. *Fool for Love: F. Scott Fitzgerald.* New York: Congdon & Weeds, 1983.

———. *Hemingway vs. Fitzgerald: The Rise and Fall of a Literary Friendship.* New York: The Overlook Press, 1999.

Fitzgerald, F. Scott. *The Beautiful and Damned.* New York: Charles Scribner's Sons, 1922.

———. *F. Scott Fitzgerald: A Life in Letters.* Edited by Matthew J. Bruccoli. New York: Simon & Schuster, 1994.

———. *The Great Gatsby.* New York: Charles Scribner's Sons, 1925.

———. *The Last Tycoon.* Edited by Edmund Wilson. New York: Charles Scribner's Sons, 1941.

———. *The Short Stories of F. Scott Fitzgerald.* Edited by Matthew J. Bruccoli. New York: Charles Scribner's Sons, 1989.

———. *Tender Is the Night: A Romance.* New York: Charles Scribner's Sons, 1934.

———. *This Side of Paradise.* New York: Charles Scribner's Sons, 1920.

Fitzgerald, Zelda. *Save Me the Waltz.* New York: Charles Scribner's Sons, 1932.

Gordon, Lois, and Alan Gordon, editors. *American Chronicle: Six Decades in American Life: 1920–1980.* New York: Atheneum, 1987.

Hemingway, Ernest. *A Moveable Feast.* New York: Charles Scribner's Sons, 1964.

———. *Selected Letters, 1917–1961.* Edited by Carlos Baker. New York: Charles Scribner's Sons, 1981.

———. *The Sun Also Rises*. New York: Charles Scribner's Sons, 1952.

Hitchens, Christopher. "The Road to West Egg." *Vanity Fair,* May 2000, 76–86.

Page, Dave, and John Koblas. *F. Scott Fitzgerald in Minnesota: Toward the Summit*. St.Cloud, MN: North Star Press of St. Cloud, Inc., 1996.

Pierpont, Claudia. "For Love and Money." *The New Yorker*, July 3, 2000, 77–83.

Untermeyer, Louis, editor. *A Treasury of Great Poems*. New York: Simon & Schuster, 1942.

In 1915 Fitzgerald, right, *spent the summer at the Montana ranch of his school friend "Sap" Donahoe.*

Selected Works Published

(This chronological list omits printed pamphlets and keepsakes, which were not for sale.)

Fie! Fie! Fi-Fi!. Cincinnati, New York, & London: The John Church Co., 1914.

The Evil Eye. Cincinnati, New York, & London: The John Church Co., 1915.

Safety First. Cincinnati, New York, & London: The John Church Co., 1916.

This Side of Paradise. New York: Charles Scribner's Sons, 1920; London: Collins, 1921.

Flappers and Philosophers. New York: Charles Scribner's Sons, 1920; London: Collins, 1922.

The Beautiful and Damned. New York: Charles Scribner's Sons, 1922; London: Collins, 1922.

Tales of the Jazz Age. New York: Charles Scribner's Sons, 1922; London: Collins, 1923.

The Vegetable. New York: Charles Scribner's Sons, 1923.

The Great Gatsby. New York: Charles Scribner's Sons, 1925; London: Chatto & Windus, 1926.

All the Sad Young Men. New York: Charles Scribner's Sons, 1926.

John Jackson's Arcady. Boston: Baker, 1928.

Tender Is the Night. New York: Charles Scribner's Sons, 1934; London: Chatto & Windus, 1934.

Taps at Reveille. New York: Charles Scribner's Sons, 1935.

The Last Tycoon. New York: Charles Scribner's Sons, 1941; London: Grey Walls, 1949.

The Crack-Up. Edited by Edmund Wilson. New York: New Directions, 1945.

The Stories of F. Scott Fitzgerald. Edited by Malcolm Cowley. New York: Charles Scribner's Sons, 1951.

Afternoon of an Author. Edited by Arthur Mizener. Princeton, NJ: Princeton University Library, 1957; New York: Charles Scribner's Sons, 1958; London: Bodley Head, 1958.

The Pat Hobby Stories. Edited by Arnold Gingrich. New York: Charles Scribner's Sons, 1962; Harmondsworth: Penguin, 1967.

The Letters of F. Scott Fitzgerald. Edited by Andrew Turnbull. New York: Charles Scribner's Sons, 1963; London: Bodley Head, 1964.

The Apprentice Fiction of F. Scott Fitzgerald. Edited by John Kuehl. New Brunswick, NJ: Rutgers University Press, 1965.

Thoughtbook of Francis Scott Key Fitzgerald. Edited by John Kuehl. Princeton, NJ: Princeton University Library, 1965.

Dearly Beloved. Iowa City, IA: Windhover Press, 1970.

F. Scott Fitzgerald in His Own Time: A Miscellany. Edited by Matthew J. Bruccoli and Jackson R. Bryer. Kent, Ohio: Kent State University Press, 1971.

Dear Scott/Dear Max. Edited by John Kuehl and Jackson R. Bryer. New York: Charles Scribner's Sons, 1971; London: Cassell, 1973.

As Ever, Scott Fitz-. Edited by Matthew J. Bruccoli and Jennifer M. Atkinson. Philadelphia and New York: J. B. Lippincott, 1972; London: Woburn, 1973.

The Basil and Josephine Stories. Edited by Jackson R. Bryer and John Kuehl. New York: Charles Scribner's Sons, 1973.

F. Scott Fitzgerald's Ledger (A Facsimile). Edited by Matthew J. Bruccoli. Washington, D.C.: Bruccoli Clark/NCR Microcard Books, 1973.

Bits of Paradise. Edited by Matthew J. Bruccoli and Scottie Fitzgerald Smith. London: Bodley Head, 1973; New York: Charles Scribner's Sons, 1974.

Preface to This Side of Paradise. Iowa City, IA: Windhover Press, 1975.

The Cruise of the Rolling Junk. Bloomfield Hills, MI & Columbia, SC: Bruccoli Clark, 1976.

F. Scott Fitzgerald's Screenplay for Eric Maria Remarque's Three Comrades. Edited by Matthew J. Bruccoli. Carbondale & Edwardsville, IL: Southern Illinois University Press, 1978.

The Notebooks of F. Scott Fitzgerald. Edited by Matthew J. Bruccoli. New York & London: Harcourt Brace Jovanovich/Bruccoli Clark, 1978.

F. Scott Fitzgerald's St. Paul Plays. Edited by Alan Margolies. Princeton, NJ: Princeton University Library, 1978.

The Price Was High. Edited by Matthew J. Bruccoli. New York & London: Harcourt Brace Jovanovich/Bruccoli Clark, 1979.

Correspondence of F. Scott Fitzgerald. Edited by Matthew J. Bruccoli and Margaret M. Duggan, with Susan Walker. New York: Random House, 1980.

Poems 1911–1940. Edited by Matthew J. Bruccoli. Bloomfield Hills, MI & Columbia, SC: Bruccoli Clark, 1981.

Online Resources

American Authors on the Web
<http://lang.nagoya-u.ac.jp/~matsuoka/AmeLit.html>
A comprehensive clearinghouse of web links that lead to sites containing information on a wide variety of contemporary and classic American authors.

American Literature Online
<http://www.missouri.edu/~engmo/amlit.html>
An array of links to websites dealing with American authors and literature.

F. Scott Fitzgerald—American Storytellers
<http://www.geocities.com//Athens/Olympus/1104/index.html>
Television dramatization based on Fitzgerald's life. Browse a biography, a reading list, behind-the-scenes notes, and related links.

F. Scott Fitzgerald Chat
<http://www.killdevilhill.com/fitzgeraldchat/wwwboard.html>
An Internet message board where web surfers can join discussions about F. Scott Fitzgerald's work, world, life, and times.

F. Scott Fitzgerald-MSN Encarta
<http://encarta.msn.com/find/Concise.asp?ti=03997000>
A brief biography of Fitzgerald, including a photo and related links.

University of South Carolina
<http://www.sc.edu/fitzgerald/>
A web venue for everything having to do with F. Scott Fitzgerald.

Further Reading

Bruccoli, Matthew J. *Fitzgerald and Hemingway: A Dangerous Friendship.* New York: Carroll & Graf, 1994.

Graham, Sheilah. *College of One.* New York: Viking, 1967.

Graham, Sheilah, and Gerold Frank. *Beloved Infidel.* New York: Holt, Rinehart & Winston, 1958.

Koblas, John J. *F. Scott Fitzgerald in Minnesota: His Homes and Haunts.* St. Paul, MN: Minnesota Historical Society Press, 1978.

Latham, John Aaron. *Crazy Sundays: F. Scott Fitzgerald in Hollywood.* New York: Viking, 1971.

LeVot, Andre. *F. Scott Fitzgerald.* Garden City, New York: Doubleday, 1983.

Mayfield, Sara. *Exiles from Paradise.* New York: Delacorte Press, 1971.

Mellow, James R. *Invented Lives.* Boston: Houghton Mifflin, 1984.

Milford, Nancy. *Zelda.* New York: Harper and Row, 1970.

Miller, Linda Patterson, ed. *Letters from the Lost Generation: Gerald and Sara Murphy and Friends.* New Brunswick, New York: Rutgers University Press, 1991.

Mizener, Arthur. *The Far Side of Paradise.* Boston: Houghton Mifflin, 1951.

Ring, Frances Kroll. *Against the Current: As I Remember F. Scott Fitzgerald.* San Francisco: Ellis/Creative Arts, 1985.

Smith, Scottie Fitzgerald, Matthew J. Bruccoli, and Joan P. Kerr, editors. *The Romantic Egoists: A Pictorial Autobiography from the Scrapbooks and Albums of F. Scott and Zelda Fitzgerald.* New York: Charles Scribner's Sons, 1974.

Tompkins, Calvin. *Living Well Is the Best Revenge.* New York: Viking, 1971.

Turnbull, Andrew. *Scott Fitzgerald.* New York: Charles Scribner's Sons, 1962.

Index

124

Other Titles in the Lerner Biographies Series

Photo Acknowledgments

Charles Scribner's Sons, front cover, p. 49; © Bettmann/CORBIS, front-back cover (background) pp. 36, 51, 78, 80, 83; Brown Brothers, pp. 2, 56, 69, 71, 74, 79, 82; Papers of the F. Scott Fitzgerald Manuscripts Division, Department of Rare Books and Special Collections, Princeton University Libraries, pp. 6, 14, 15, 16, 18, 20, 23, 26, 28, 33, 34, 39, 41, 42, 47, 50, 54, 61, 62, 70, 72, 84, 91, 92, 107, 109, 119; © Culver Pictures, pp. 9, 13, 44, 64, 89, 94; Minnesota Historical Society, pp. 10, 12, 22, 25, 59, 66, 67; Library of Congress, pp. 30 (LC-USZ62-125530), 97 (LC-USZ62-75217), 102 (LC-USZ62-88103); The University Archives, Seeley G. Mudd Manuscript Library, Princeton University Libraries, p. 31; © CORBIS, p. 46; © George Eastman House/ Nickolas Muray/Archive Photos, p. 58; © Fox Photos/Archive Photos, pp. 77, 100; John F. Kennedy Library, p. 87; © Hulton-Deutsch Collection/CORBIS, pp. 96, 110.

All attempts were made to contact the copyright holder. If a photograph appears in the book without credit, please contact Lerner Publishing Group.

About the Author

Caroline Evensen Lazo has written numerous biographies of men and women who have illuminated the world and enriched our lives. Her books include *Arthur Ashe* and *Alice Walker: Freedom Writer*—both Notable Social Studies Trade Books for Young People, selected by the National Council for Social Studies— as well as *Gloria Steinem: Feminist Extraordinaire* and *Leonard Bernstein: In Love with Music.* Ms. Lazo graduated from the University of Minnesota and attended the International School at the University of Oslo, Norway, the home of her paternal ancestors. Her professional writing career began with the publication of "A Time to Fail . . . A Time to Succeed," a *Parents Magazine* cover story concerning the effects of home life on a child's performance in school. Her own three children remain the inspiration behind all of her books. Ms. Lazo grew up in Minneapolis, and, like F. Scott Fitzgerald, spent her childhood summers at beautiful White Bear Lake. Years later, she served on the local committee of the Sixth International Conference of the F. Scott Fitzgerald Society, held in St. Paul, Minnesota.